Learning By Example Using C
-- Programming the *miniDRAGON-Plus2*™ Using *CodeWarrior*™

Richard E. Haskell
Darrin M. Hanna

Oakland University, Rochester, Michigan

LBE Books
Rochester, MI

ISBN 978-0-9801337-2-1

Published by LBE Books, LLC
360 South Street
Suite 202
Rochester, MI 48307

www.lbebooks.com

Preface

Microcontrollers such as the Freescale MC9SDG256 are remarkable devices. They contain not only a sophisticated microprocessor with a rich set of instructions and addressing modes, but also contain built-in RAM, EEPROM, and flash memory as well as numerous useful I/O ports, including parallel I/O, several different types of serial I/O, timers, and A/D converters.

This extensive list of features makes the programming of these microcontrollers, particularly using assembly language, a daunting task. A quick look at the many textbooks (or the many datasheets) that describe these microcontrollers will confirm this. These books and datasheets spend a great deal of time explaining how to program the many I/O registers to perform the wide variety of different I/O tasks. However, it is usually something fairly simple that you are trying to do; e.g. turn on a light, read a switch, turn on a motor at some speed, read the value of an A/D converter, or measure some time interval. If you just want to learn how to do these simple things without getting bogged down in the minutia of the microcontrollers I/O and internal operation, then this book is for you.

Compare this book to your automobile. Most of us want to use our car to get from one place to another easily and in comfort. We don't want to have to learn how to design and build an internal combustion engine or automatic transmission in order to drive our car. By the same token you should not have to learn a particular assembly language or the details of what each bit in dozens of different I/O registers do in order to quickly and effectively program a microcontroller to do what you want it to do. Tnis book will show you how to do just that.

Of course, some people like to look under the hood of their car to see how things really work. If you really want to see how the assembly language routines that we provide for you actually work you can study the entire source listing that is included in our stationery project. But it isn't necessary to get your microcontroller to work.

This book assumes no previous knowledge of either microcontrollers or C. We will use a particular microcontroller, the Freescale MC9S12DG256, on a popular, low-cost development board, the miniDRAGON-Plus2™ from Wytec, Inc. The reason for using this microcontroller is that it is one of the more powerful in the popular HCS12 family with lots of I/O capabilities, and the reasons for using the miniDRAGON-Plus2 in addition to its low cost, are the small footprint that makes it suitable for embedded projects, the convenient female headers for connecting to your circuits on the protoboard, and the built-in connectors for an LCD display and keypad. There is also an on-board speaker, a built-in H-bridge for driving motors, convenient headers for connecting servos and an accelerometer board available from Wytec, and female headers for connecting to your circuits on the built-in protoboard. You will quickly be able to do lots of fun stuff with this board. A companion book for use with Wytec's DRAGON12-Plus board is also available from LBE Books (www.lbebooks.com).

In this book you will learn to write programs in C and compile them to HCS12 code using CodeWarrior™, an industry-strength integrated development environment for microcontrollers. CodeWarrior itself can be daunting, but we will make it easy for you to learn what you need to quickly get your microcontroller to work. We do this by providing you with an *LBE_miniDRAGON_Plus2* Stationery project from which you can easily build your own particular application. This project will contain an assembly language file that we have written to do all the low-level interaction with the I/O registers. You can then concentrate on driving your car in C rather than wasting your time figuring out how the internal combustion engine works! So let's get started.

Many colleagues, students and reviewers have influenced the development of this book. Their stimulating discussions, probing questions, and critical comments are greatly appreciated. Special thanks go to Michael Latcha and Osamah Rawashdeh with whom we have had many useful discussions related to the contents of this book.

Richard E. Haskell
Darrin M. Hanna

Learning By Example Using C
-- Programming the miniDRAGON-Plus2™ Using CodeWarrior™

Table of Contents

Introduction

Microcontrollers and C

The HCS12 is the latest family of Freescale microcontrollers and is a direct descendent of the original Motorola 68HC11 and the more recent 68HC12. In this book you will learn how to program the MC9S12DG256 microcontroller that is on the Wytec miniDRAGON-Plus2 board by studying 21 detailed examples of programs written in C using the industry-standard CodeWarrior development system. To make it as easy as possible we have provided a stationery project that you can build upon that includes a large collection of built-in assembly language routines to access all of the various I/O functions of the MC9S12DG256. You will access these routines through C function calls.

From Microprocessors to Microcontrollers

A major revolution in the computer industry has taken place in the past thirty years. The making of the first microprocessor was made possible by the remarkable development of integrated circuits during the 1960s. This technology allowed hundreds and then thousands of transistors to be etched onto a single piece of silicon. This led to the design of integrated circuits in which more and more logic elements were incorporated into a single chip. In 1969 Intel undertook a contract to develop a set of integrated circuits that could be used to make a programmable electronic calculator. Instead of developing yet another special purpose integrated circuit with only a limited function, Intel chose to produce a more general purpose device, the 4004 microprocessor, which could be programmed to perform many different functions. This first microprocessor had only four data lines over which both address information and data had to be sent to memory devices. Intel put this chip on the market in 1971 as part of a four chip set that formed a micro-programmable computer. The 4004 had many limitations and the following year Intel introduced the 8008 and two years later the 8080 which became widely used in a host of different applications. In 1975 Motorola produced its first microprocessor -- the 6800.

The 6800 had 8 data lines (called a *data bus*) and 16 address lines (called an *address bus*). This means that it could address $2^{16} = 65{,}536$ different memory addresses, each containing 8 bits, or one byte of data. The heart of the 6800 was its CPU, or central processing unit, sometimes referred to as an MPU, or microprocessor unit. The CPU contained the registers and logic to execute the instruction set of the 6800. The 6800 registers included two 8-bit accumulators (*A* and *B*), a 16-bit index register (*X*), a 16-bit stack pointer (*SP*), a 16-bit program counter (*PC*), and an 8-bit condition-code register

(*CCR*). Thus, the first microprocessors consisted only of a CPU that could address external memory as shown in Figure 1.

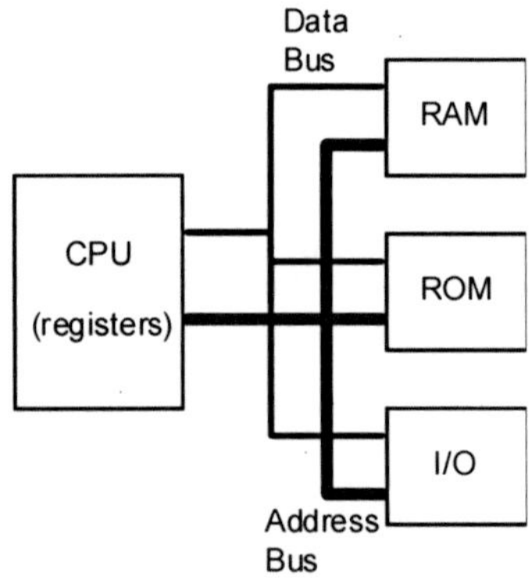

Figure 1 A microprocessor (CPU) connected to external memory

The external memory shown in Figure 1 consists of read-write memory (RAM), read-only memory (ROM), and input/output memory (I/O). Typically the I/O memory consists of dedicated special-purpose devices for performing such operations as parallel I/O, serial I/O, timer functions, and analog-to-digital (A/D) conversion. These I/O devices contain registers that look like memory locations to the CPU. The RAM in Figure 1 could be either static RAM (SRAM) or dynamic RAM (DRAM). Dynamic RAM can contain more bytes of memory than static RAM for the same size chip, but requires additional circuitry to refresh the data periodically to keep it from being lost. Other types of memory devices that might be connected to the address and data busses in Figure 1 include erasable programmable read-only memory (EPROM), electrically-erasable programmable read-only memory (EEPROM), and flash EEPROM. Both flash EEPROM and EEPROM are non-volatile memory that will maintain their data when power is removed. Individual bytes can be erased and programmed in EEPROM while flash EEPROMs normally require erasing the entire memory array at one time.

As integrated circuit technology developed over the years one of the trends has been the development of faster and more complex microprocessors such as the Intel 80x86 and Pentium and the Motorola 680x0 and PowerPC. These microprocessors are in many of the popular desktop computers used in offices all over the world. Another trend has been to package more and more functionality onto a single chip. The Motorola 6801 was introduced in 1978 and included a small amount of RAM and ROM as well as parallel and serial I/O on a single chip. The following year Motorola introduced an EPROM version of the 6801, the 68701, as well as the first of the low-cost 6805 family of microcontrollers.

The first 68HC11 was introduced by Motorola in 1985. This 8-bit microcontroller (the A8 part) contained on a single chip the CPU11 microprocessor, 8 Kbytes of ROM, 256 bytes of RAM, 512 bytes of EEPROM, up to 38 parallel I/O lines, a 16-bit timer that includes 3 input captures and 5 output compares, a synchronous serial peripheral interface (SPI), an asynchronous serial communications interface (SCI), and an 8-channel, 8-bit A/D converter. Since 1985 over five dozen different 68HC11 parts have been introduced by Motorola. These parts differ in the types and amounts of on-board resources that are included in the chip.

In 1997 Motorola introduced the 68HC12 as an enhanced 68HC11. It is upward compatible with the 68HC11 (but not at the object code level). It has a greatly enhanced central processing unit (CPU12) that has several new instructions and addressing modes designed to make it easier to support higher-level languages. Programs run significantly faster on a 68HC12 for several reasons. The typical clock speed was increased from 2 MHz on a 68HC11 to 8 MHz on a 68HC12. The number of clock cycles required to execute many of the instructions was reduced on the 68HC12. In addition, the new instructions and addressing modes require fewer instructions to perform the same task. This means that not only do programs run faster, but they also take up less memory space.

In 2002 Motorola introduced the HCS12 family of microcontrollers, which are a direct upgrade of the 68HC12 family. The Motorola Semiconductor Division was spun off as Freescale in 2004. The MC9S12DG256 microcontroller that is on the miniDRAGON-Plus2 board has 256K bytes of flash EEPROM, 12K bytes of RAM, 4K bytes of EEPROM, two 8-channel, 10-bit analog-to-digital (A/D) converters, two asynchronous serial communication interfaces (SCI), three serial peripheral interfaces (SPI), an 8-channel timer module that supports output compare and input capture, an 8-channel pulse-width modulator (PWM), 29 discrete digital I/O channels, and comprehensive interrupt functions. We will cover all of these I/O functions in this book. The MC9S12DG256 microcontroller has additional functions not covered in this book including two CAN 2.0 modules, an Inter-IC bus, and a digital Byte Data Link Controller (BDLC). The part can operate up to 25 MHz and we will run all of our programs at a clock speed of 24 MHz.

A block diagram of a typical HCS12 microcontroller is shown in Figure 2. In the single-chip mode (which is what the miniDRAGON-Plus2 uses) the entire program is stored in the flash memory and the only contact with the outside world is through the various peripheral lines connected to the timer, parallel I/O, SPI, SCI, or A/D converter. An HCS12 microcontroller can also operate in an expanded multiplexed mode in which the parallel I/O lines become multiplexed address and data busses that can be used to address external memory.

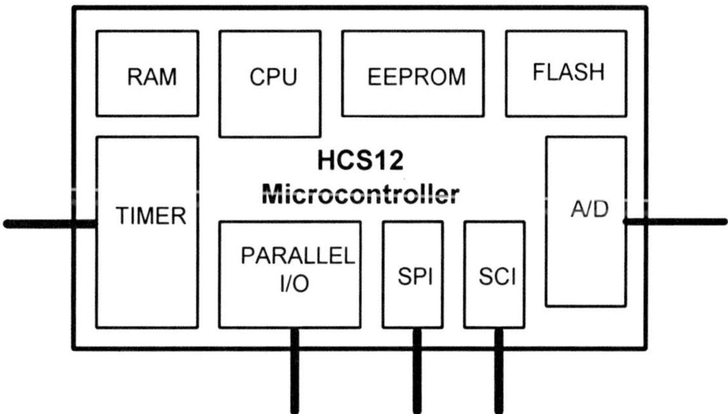

Figure 2 Block diagram of an HCS12 microcontroller

Programming Microcontrollers in C

Traditionally microcontrollers have been programmed in assembly language. The advantage of assembly language is that it is closest to the hardware and can execute programs most efficiently. The disadvantage of assembly language is that it is not portable. Every time you change to a different microcontroller you have to rewrite all of your programs. In addition it generally takes longer to say something in assembly language than it does in a high-level language and therefore it generally takes longer to write assembly language programs than it does to write high-level programs. For these reasons the trend in recent years is to program microcontrollers in a high-level language – the most popular being C .

However, even when programming a microcontroller in C you still have to get close to the hardware to program all of the I/O registers. Thus, even C programs for microcontrollers can be long and intimidating. In this book we have tried to get the best of both worlds. We have written over eighty assembly language routines that access all of the important I/O functions of the Freescale MC9S12DG256 microcontroller and have included these routines in the file *main.asm* that is part of the stationery project *LBE_miniDRAGON_Plus2* upon which you can build all of your C programs. You can access any of these assembly language routines by simple C function calls in your C program. A list of all of these C function calls is given in Appendix C.

The assembly language routines are designed specifically to access the hardware on the Wytec miniDRAGON-Plus2 board shown in Fig. 3. This board contains the Freescale MC9S12DG256 microcontroller surrounded by four convenient female headers that bring out all of the I/O ports. This makes it easy to interface to your own I/O circuitry on the attached protoboard. In addition the board contains a single 7-segment display, two pushbutton switches, a potentiometer for reading in an analog voltage between 0 and 5 volts, a connector for a liquid crystal display (LCD), and a connector for a hex keypad. Example programs in this book show how to access all of these I/O functions and much more.

Therefore, let's get started!

Figure 3 The Wytec miniDRAGON-Plus2 board

Example 1

7-Segment Display: Parallel Port

In this example we will show how to turn on the segments of the 7-segment display on the miniDRAGON-Plus2 board. As in all of our examples we will first show you how to do it entirely in C, and then we will show how to do it using C calls to our built-in assembly language routines. Using these built-in assembly language routines will make your C programs much shorter and easier to write.

1.1 MC9S12DG256 Parallel I/O Ports

The MC9S12DG256 registers associated with parallel I/O are listed in Table 1.1. Each of these ports (except *PORTAD0* and *PORTAD1*) has a data register and a data direction register of the type shown in Figure 1.1. Each pin of an I/O port can be either an input or an output depending on the bits in the corresponding data direction register as shown in Figure 1.1.

Table 1.1 Parallel Ports in the MC9SDG256

Port	Port Name	DDR Name	Available Pins	MiniDragon-Plus2 use
Port T	PTT	DDRT	7:0	Speaker
Port S	PTS	DDRS	7:0	SCI(1:0)
Port M	PTM	DDRM	7:0	LCD
Port P	PTP	DDRP	7:0	
Port H	PTH	DDRH	7:0	7-Seg Display
Port J	PTJ	DDRJ	7,6,1,0	
Port AD0	PORTAD0	Input only	7:0	Switches, pot
Port AD1	PORTAD1	Input only	7:0	
Port A	PORTA	DDRA	7:0	Keypad
Port B	PORTB	DDRB	7:0	
Port E	PORTE	DDRE	7:0	Mode, XIRQ
Port K	PORTK	DDRK	7, 5:0	

Most of the I/O ports listed in Table 1 have alternate or special optional functions many of which we will consider in later examples. When the pins of an I/O port are not being used for one of these alternate functions they can be used as general purpose I/O pins.

There are several different operating modes for the MC9S12DG256 including a single-chip mode and expanded external memory modes. In the expanded external memory modes ports A and B are used for multiplexed address and data busses. The miniDRAGON-Plus2 board operates in the single-chip mode, so that ports A and B are available for parallel I/O. Port A is connected to the keypad connector.

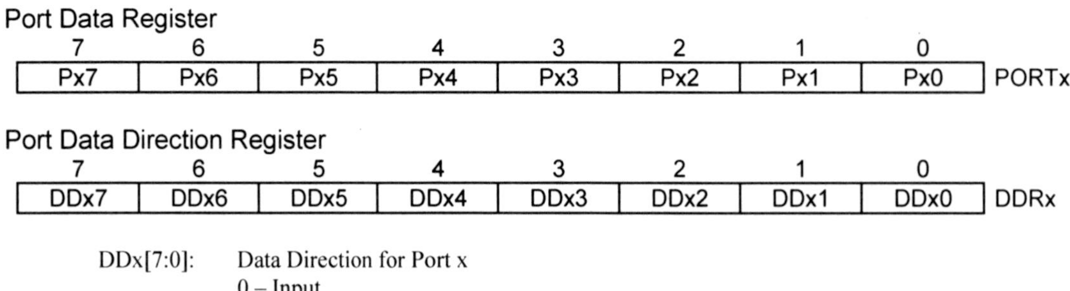

DDx[7:0]: Data Direction for Port x
0 – Input
1 – Output

Figure 1.1 Registers associated with parallel I/O ports

1.2 7-Segment Displays

Port H is connected to the 7-segment display. In this example we will write two C programs to turn on every other segment. A light emitting diode (LED) emits light when current flows through it in the positive direction as shown in Fig. 1.2. Current flows through the LED when the voltage on the *anode* side (the wide side of the black triangle) is made higher than the voltage on the *cathode* side (the straight line connected to the apex of the black triangle). When current flows through a lighted LED the forward voltage across the LED is typically between +1.5 and +2.0 volts. If voltage V2 in Fig. 1.2 is less than or equal to voltage V1 then no current can flow through the LED and therefore no light will be emitted. If voltage V2 is greater than voltage V1 then current will flow through the resistor *R* and the LED. The resistor is used to limit the amount of current that flows through the LED. Typical currents needed to light LEDs range from 2 to 15 milliamps.

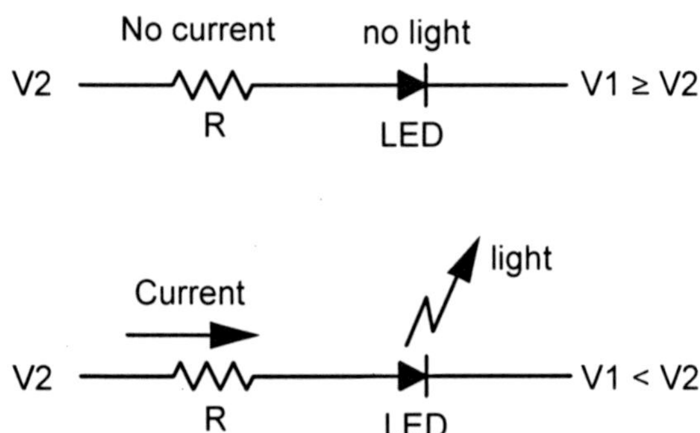

Figure 1.2 Turning on an LED

There are two different ways that an I/O pin of a microcontroller can be used to turn on an LED. The first is to connect the pin to V1 in Fig. 1.2 and to connect V2 to a constant voltage. Bringing the pin (V1) low will then turn on the LED. To turn off the LED the output pin would be brought high. This voltage should be equal to V2 to make sure no current flows through the LED. The second method is to connect the pin to V2 in Fig. 4.2 and to

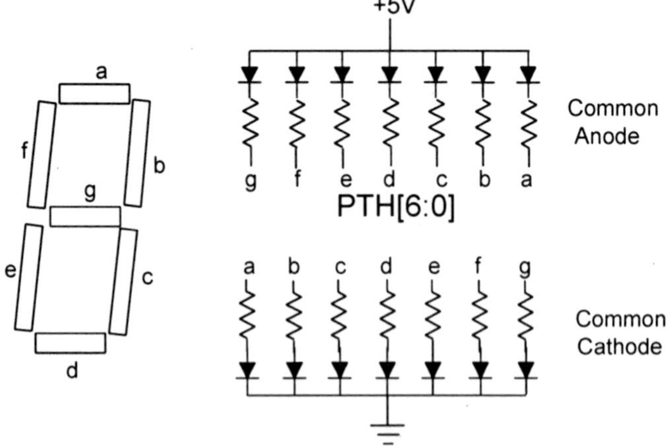

Figure 1.3 A 7-segment display contains seven light emitting diodes (LEDs)

connect V1 to ground. Bringing the pin (V2) high will then turn on the LED. To turn off the LED the output pin would be brought low.

Seven LEDs can be arranged in a pattern to form different digits as shown in Fig. 1.3. Digital watches use similar 7-segment displays using liquid crystals rather than LEDs. The red digits on digital clocks are LEDs. Seven segment displays come in two flavors: common anode and common cathode. A common anode 7-segment display has all of the anodes tied together while a common cathode 7-segment display has all the cathodes tied together as shown in Fig. 1.3.

The miniDRAGON-Plus2 board has a common-anode 7-segment display. This means that all the anodes are tied together and connected to +5V. The output pins 6:0 of Port H are connected through a 1 kΩ current-limiting resistor to each of the anodes, *g* – *a*. In the common-anode case, an output 0 will turn on a segment and an output 1 will turn it off.

1.3 Example 1a – Write to Port H

Follow the steps in the tutorial in Appendix A to set up CodeWarrior and create a new project called *Example1* where you select the stationery file LBE_miniDRAGON_Plus2. When you open the file *main.c* in the *Source* folder you should see the program shown in Listing 1.1.

Listing 1.1 Example 1a

```
// Example 1a: Turn on every other segment on 7-segment
display
#include <hidef.h>            /* common defines and macros */
#include <mc9s12dg256.h>      /* derivative information */
#pragma LINK_INFO DERIVATIVE "mc9s12dg256b"

#include "main_asm.h"   /* interface to the assembly module */


void main(void) {
/* put you own code here */
  PLL_init();          // set system clock frequency to 24 MHz
  DDRH  = 0xff;        // Port H is output
  PTH   = 0xAA;        // switch on every other segment
  for(;;) {}      /* wait forever */
}
```

The three lines following the comment `/* put you own code here */` will do the following:

1. The statement `PLL_init();` will set the system bus frequency to 24 MHz. We will desribe this statement more in Example 2.

2. The statement `DDRH = 0xff;` will set all bits in data direction register H to 1 and therefore to all outputs. The notation *0x* means that *ff* is a hexadecimal number equal to the binary number 11111111.

3. The statement `PTH = 0xAA;` will set the bits in port H to 10101010 and therefore turn on segments *a*, *c*, *e*, and *g* shown in Fig. 1.3. Remember, a 0 turns a segment on and a 1 turns a segment off. The bits in port H are connected to the segments of the 7-segment display as shown in Fig. 1.4.

4. The statement `for(;;) {}` will just loop on itself forever. We will describe the use of the C *for* loop in more detail in Example 2

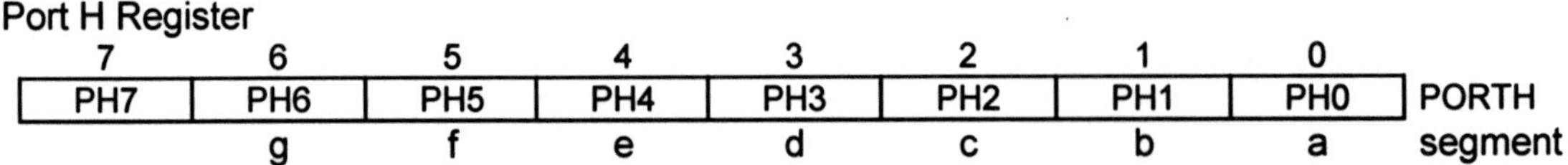

Figure 1.4 Connections of Port H to 7-segment display

1.4 Example 1b – Function calls for 7-segment display

Instead of having to remember that the 7-segment display is connected to Port H we have written two assembly language routines that are called by the two C function calls shown in Table 1.1. These assembly language routines are always available to you when you set up an *LBE_miniDRAGON_Plus2* stationery project. Listing 1.2 shows how you can modify the program in Listing 1.1 to produce the same result.

Table 1.1 C function calls for turning on the 7-segment display

C Function Call	Meaning
`seg7_enable();`	Sets DDRH to outputs and clears all segments
`seg7_on(int);`	Stores the lower 8 bits of the integer *int* in Port H
`seg7_off();`	Turn off all 7 segments by clearing Port H

Listing 1.2 Example 1b

```
// Example 1b: 7-Segment Display
#include <hidef.h>              /* common defines and macros */
#include <mc9s12dg256.h>        /* derivative information */
#pragma LINK_INFO DERIVATIVE "mc9s12dg256b"

#include "main_asm.h"    /* interface to the assembly module */

void main(void) {
  PLL_init();          // set system clock frequency to 24 MHz
  seg7_enable();          // enable 7-segment display
  seg7_on(0xAA);          // switch on every other segment

  for(;;) {} /* wait forever */
}
```

PROBLEMS

1.1 Modify Listing 1.2 to turn on all segments.

1.2 Modify Listing 1.2 to display the letter L.

1.3 Modify Listing 1.2 to display the letter H.

1.4 Modify Listing 1.2 to display the letter P.

1.5 Modify Listing 1.2 to display the letter A.

1.6 Modify Listing 1.2 to display the letter E.

Example 2

Blinking 7-Segment Display: Delay Loops

In this example we will show how to blink the segments of the 7-segment display on the miniDRAGON-Plus2 board. We will first show you how to make a delay loop in C, and then we will provide a new C function call to a built-in delay routine written in assembly language.

2.1 Example 2a – A Delay Loop in C

We will generate a delay by making a simple software delay loop. A more accurate way of producing a delay is to use the timer module in the MC9S12DG256. We will look at how to do this in future examples. Listing 2.1 shows how to make a software delay using two nested *for* loops.

Listing 2.1 Example 2a

```
// Example 2a: Blinking 7-Segment Display
#include <hidef.h>          /* common defines and macros */
#include <mc9s12dg256.h>    /* derivative information */
#pragma LINK_INFO DERIVATIVE "mc9s12dg256b"

#include "main_asm.h"   /* interface to the assembly module */

void delay(void);

void main(void) {
  PLL_init();       // set system clock frequency to 24 MHz
  seg7_enable();          // enable 7-segment display
  while(1){
    seg7_on(0x00);        // switch on all segments
    delay();
    seg7_on(0xFF);        // switch off all segments
    delay();
  }
}

void delay() {
  int i,j;
  for(i = 0; i < 500; i++) {
    for(j = 0; j < 5999; j++) {
    }
  }
}
```

The C *for* loop has the following general form

```
for(initial_index; terminal_index; increment) {
     statements;
}
```

In the inner *for* loop in the *delay()* function in Listing 2.1 the *initial_index* is defined by the statement `j = 0;` where `j` is a 16-bit integer declared along with `i` in the statement

```
int i,j;.
```

The *terminal_index* in the inner *for* loop is defined by the statement `j < 5999;` and the *increment* is defined by the statement `j++`. The statement `j++` is equivalent to `j = j + 1` which just increments `j` by 1. Thus, in this *for* loop the index `j` starts at 0, the statements between the braces {...} are executed (there are no statements in the inner *for* loop in Listing 2.1), the index `j` is incremented by 1, and the statements between the braces are executed again. This process continues until the *terminal_index* is reached, or in this case when the statement `j < 5999;` is false, i.e. when `j` gets incremented to 5999. Thus, this *for* loop will execute 5999 times. We chose this number because it is the same as the number of times we go through the inner loop of our assembly language delay routine to produce a 1 millisecond delay. The delay in the C *for* loop will be slightly longer because the *for* loop gets compiled to assembly language instructions that take a few more clock cycles than in our assembly language delay loop.

The inner *for* loop in the *delay()* function in Listing 2.1 will execute 500 times and each time through this outer for loop the inner for loop will execute 5999 times. Thus, the total number of times through the inner loop before the *delay()* function exits will be 500 x 5999 = 2,999,500. The bus clock frequency of the microcontroller is 24 MHz so if the inner *for* loop took 4 clock cycles, then the total delay time will be 4 x 2,999,500 / 24,000,000 = 0.5 seconds.

The MC9S12DG256 contains phase-locked loop (PLL) circuitry that CodeWarrior uses to set the bus frequency to 24 MHz. Thus, when you download a program to the flash memory using CodeWarrior your program will be running at 24 MHz. However, when you move the left slide switch, S7, to RUN and press the reset button, your program will normally run at a lower bus clock frequency that depends on the crystal on your board. To keep the frequency at 24 MHz when our programs are executed out of reset we must include the statement *PLL_init()* at the beginning of our programs that will initialize the PLL to produce a PLL (oscillator) frequency of 48 MHz which results in a bus frequency of 24 MHz. Thus, the program in Listing 2.1 will change the blinking digit every half second even when you move the slide switch to RUN and press reset. The default stationery file *main.c* that comes up when you create a new project contains this *PLL_init()* function at the beginning of the program. You should keep this function call in all of your programs so that your program will always run at 24 MHz even out of reset.

Before the main program in Listing 2.1 we have included the *delay()* function prototype declaration

```
void delay(void);
```

The first *void* in this statement indicates that this function does not return any value to the calling program. The second *void* in the parentheses indicates that there are no parameters to be passed from the calling program to the function. All functions that you use in your C programs must have a prototype declaration. These are often grouped together in a separate *.h* file, but you can also include them at the beginning of the program as we have done here.

The main program in Listing 2.1 first enables the 7-segment display and then enters a *while* loop. The C *while* loop has the following general form

```
while(expression) {
        statements;
}
```

When the while loop is executed the *expression* in the parentheses is evaluated, and if it is *true*, the statements between the braces {...} are executed, and then the *expression* in the parentheses is evaluated again. As long as the *expression* is true the statements will be executed again. When the *expression* becomes false, the *while* loop is exited without executing the statements again. A value of zero for the expression is taken to be false, and a non-zero value is taken to be true. Therefore, in the statement *while(1)* in Listing 2.1 the expression is always true, so the *while* loop is never exited. We use this statement to continually execute the statements within the *while* loop forever.

Within the while loop we first turn on all segments of the 7-segment display, delay approximately half a second, turn off all segments of the 7-segment display, and then delay approximately half a second again. This process repeats endlessly, causing the display to blink on and off about every second. Try it.

2.2 Example 1b – Function call for delay loop

Instead of having to write your own delay loop in C we have written an assembly language routine that is called by the C function call shown in Table 2.1. This assembly language routine is always available to you when you set up an *LBE_miniDRAGON_Plus2* stationery project. Listing 2.2 shows how you can modify the program in Listing 2.1 to produce the same result. Try it.

Table 2.1 C function call delaying *n* milliseconds

C Function Call	Meaning
`ms_delay(int n);`	Delay *n* milliseconds

Listing 2.2 Example 2b

```
// Example 2b: Blinking 7-Segment Display - ms_delay(ms)
#include <hidef.h>              /* common defines and macros */
#include <mc9s12dg256.h>        /* derivative information */
#pragma LINK_INFO DERIVATIVE "mc9s12dg256b"

#include "main_asm.h"    /* interface to the assembly module */

void main(void) {
  PLL_init();         // set system clock frequency to 24 MHz
  seg7_enable();            // enable 7-segment display
  while(1){
    seg7_on(0x00);            // switch on all segments
    ms_delay(500);              // half-second delay
    seg7_on(0xFF);              // switch off all segments
    ms_delay(500);              // half-second delay
  }
}
```

PROBLEMS

2.1 Modify Listing 2.2 to blink a 2 every 2 seconds.

2.2 Modify Listing 2.2 to blink a 5 every 0.5 seconds.

2.3 Modify Listing 2.2 to blink a 1 every 0.25 seconds.

2.4 Modify Listing 2.2 to blink a 3 every 3 seconds.

2.5 Modify Listing 2.2 to blink a 5 every 0.2 seconds.

2.6 Modify Listing 2.2 to blink a 4 every 4 seconds.

Example 3

7-Segment Display: Hex Counter

In this example we will show how to have the 7-segment display on the miniDRAGON-Plus2 board count in hex from 0 to F continually. We will first show you how to do this entirely in C, and then we will provide a new C function call to display any hex digit.

3.1 Example 3a – A 7-Segment Decoder

We have seen that the miniDRAGON-Plus2 board has a common-cathode 7-segment display connected to Port H. The table shown in Fig. 3.1 shows output anode values for each segment *a* – *g* needed to display all hex digits, *D*, from 0 – F. Remember a 0 turns a segment *on* and a 1 turns a segment *off.*

Listing 3.1 shows how we can create a table of the hex codes in Fig. 3.1 by using a constant character array called *seg7tbl*[]. The type declaration *char* defines each element of the array *seg7tbl*[] to be an 8-bit byte. The type qualifier *const* defines each of these array elements to be a constant that can't be changed in the program. Note how the braces {..} are used in the array definition to define the 16 constant hex codes given in Fig. 3.1. Also note that the type declarations for *seg7tbl*[] and the integer *i* used in the for loop must precede the function call *PLL_init*().

D	g	f	e	d	c	b	a	code
0	1	0	0	0	0	0	0	40
1	1	1	1	1	0	0	1	79
2	0	1	0	0	1	0	0	24
3	0	1	1	0	0	0	0	30
4	0	0	1	1	0	0	1	19
5	0	0	1	0	0	1	0	12
6	0	0	0	0	0	1	0	02
7	1	1	1	1	0	0	0	78
8	0	0	0	0	0	0	0	00
9	0	0	1	0	0	0	0	10
A	0	0	0	1	0	0	0	08
b	0	0	0	0	0	1	1	03
C	1	0	0	0	1	1	0	46
d	0	1	0	0	0	0	1	21
E	0	0	0	0	1	1	0	06
F	0	0	0	1	1	1	0	0E

a
f
b
g
e
c
d

Figure 3.1 Segment values required to display hex digits 0 – F

In the *while* loop in Listing 3.1 there is a *for* loop with an index *i* that goes from 0 to 15. Each time through this *for* loop the output of Port H is set to `seg7tbl[i]` which will output the proper hex code corresponding to the hex digit *i*. Note that the square brackets [] are used to indicate array elements in C. The second statement in the *for* loop is a short delay (about half a second) before the next digit is displayed. Once all 16 digits have been displayed the *while*(1) loop will just keep counting again. Try it.

Listing 3.1 Example 3a

```
// Example 3a: 7-Segment Decoder - C version
#include <hidef.h>            /* common defines and macros */
#include <mc9s12dg256.h>      /* derivative information */
#pragma LINK_INFO DERIVATIVE "mc9s12dg256b"

#include "main_asm.h"   /* interface to the assembly module */

void delay(void);

void main(void) {
  const char seg7tbl[] = {
        0x40,0x79,0x24,0x30,
        0x19,0x12,0x02,0x78,
        0x00,0x10,0x08,0x03,
        0x46,0x21,0x06,0x0E
  };
  int i;

  PLL_init();        // set system clock frequency to 24 MHz
  seg7_enable();          // enable 7-segment display
  while(1){
    for(i = 0; i < 16; i++) {
       PTH = seg7tbl[i];
       delay();
    }
  }
}

void delay() {
  int i,j;
  for(i = 0; i < 500; i++) {
    for(j = 0; j < 6248; j++) {
    }
  }
}
```

3.2 Example 3b – A function call to display hex digits

Instead of having to make your own 7-segment decoder table we have written an assembly language routine that is called by the C function call shown in Table 3.1. This assembly language routine is always available to you when you set up an *LBE_miniDRAGON_Plus2* stationery project. Listing 3.2 shows how you can modify the program in Listing 3.1 to produce the same result. Try it.

Table 3.1 C function call for displaying hex digits

C Function Call	Meaning
`seg7dec(int i);`	Display the hex digit *i* on the 7-segment display

Listing 3.2 Example 3b

```
// Example 3b: 7-Segment Decoder - seg7dec(i)
#include <hidef.h>           /* common defines and macros */
#include <mc9s12dg256.h>     /* derivative information */
#pragma LINK_INFO DERIVATIVE "mc9s12dg256b"

#include "main_asm.h"   /* interface to the assembly module */

void main(void) {
  int i;
  PLL_init();        // set system clock frequency to 24 MHz
  seg7_enable();         // enable 7-segment display
  while(1){
    for(i = 0; i < 16; i++) {
       seg7dec(i);
       ms_delay(500);
    }
  }
}
```

PROBLEMS

3.1 Modify Listing 3.2 to count only the even hex digits.

3.2 Modify Listing 3.2 to count only the odd hex digits.

3.3 Modify Listing 3.2 to count down from F to 0.

3.4 Modify Listing 3.2 to count down only the even hex digits.

3.5 Modify Listing 3.2 to count down only the odd hex digits.

3.6 Modify Listing 3.2 to count only hex digits that are divisible by 3.

Example 4

7-Segment Display: Single Segments

In this example we will show how to turn on and off individual segments in the 7-segment display on the miniDRAGON-Plus2 board. We will first show you how to do this entirely in C, and then we will provide new C function calls to do this.

4.1 Example 4a – Shorthand Assignment Operators

Consider the C program shown in Listing 4.1 which first turns on segments *a*, *g*, and *d* in turn, and then turns them off in turn.

Listing 4.1 Example 4a

```
// Example 4a: Single segments in 7-Segment Display
#include <hidef.h>            /* common defines and macros */
#include <mc9s12dg256.h>      /* derivative information */
#pragma LINK_INFO DERIVATIVE "mc9s12dg256b"

#include "main_asm.h"   /* interface to the assembly module */

void delay(void);

void main(void) {
  PLL_init();       // set system clock frequency to 24 MHz
  seg7_enable();        // enable 7-segment display
  while(1){
    PTH &= 0xFE;        // turn on segment a
    delay();
    PTH &= 0xBF;        // turn on segment g
    delay();
    PTH &= 0xF7;        // turn on segment d
    delay();
    PTH |= 0x01;        // turn off segment a
    delay();
    PTH |= 0x40;        // turn off segment g
    delay();
    PTH |= 0x08;        // turn off segment d
    delay();
  }
}

void delay() {
  int i,j;
  for(i = 0; i < 500; i++) {
    for(j = 0; j < 6248; j++) {
    }
  }
}
```

What do you need to do to turn *on* a single segment? We know that writing a 0 to the bit position in PTH corresponding to a particular segment (see Fig. 4.1) will turn on that segment. For example, writing a 0 to PH6 in Fig. 4.1 will turn on segment *g*. But when you do this you don't want to change any other segments. For example, if only segment *a* is on then PTH will have the value 01111110. Now to turn on segment *g* while leaving segment *a* on we must write the value 00111110 to PTH. The way to turn on segment *g* while leaving all other segments unchanged is to first read PTH, then AND it with the mask 10111111 (or 0xBF), and finally write the resulting value back in PTH. A C statement that will do this is

```
PTH = PTH & 0xBF;                                   (4.1)
```

where & is the C operator for a bitwise AND operation. That is, each bit in PTH is ANDed with the corresponding bit in the hex value 0xBF. A shorthand way of writing the C statement (4.1) is

```
PTH &= 0xBF;                                        (4.2)
```

Thus, statements (4.1) and (4.2) are equivalent where &= is called a shorthand assignment operator. Other C operators and shorthand assignment operators are shown in Table 4.1.

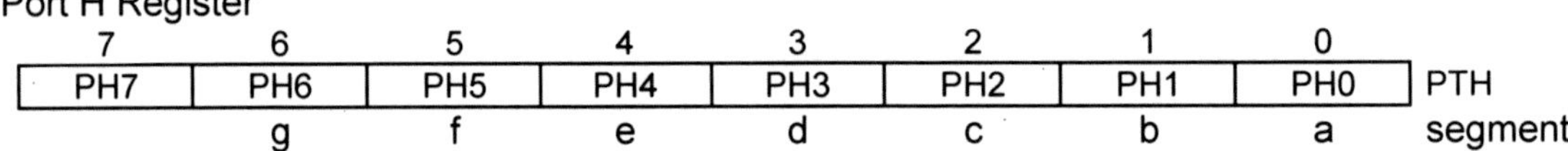

Figure 4.1 Connections of Port H to 7-segment display

Table 4.1 Operators and Assignment Operators

Operator	Description	Assignment Operator
&	Bitwise AND	&=
|	Bitwise OR	|=
^	Bitwise XOR	^=
+	Addition	+=
-	Subtraction	-=
*	Multiplication	*=
/	Division	/=
%	Modulus	%=

What do you need to do to turn *off* a single segment? It should be clear that you need to write a 1 to the corresponding bit position in PTH without changing any other bit. ORing a bit with 0 will keep the bit unchanged, while ORing a bit with 1 will force the bit to 1. Therefore, for example, to turn off segment *d* we would need to OR PTH with 00001000 (or 0x08). We can do this by using either the C statement

```
PTH = PTH | 0x08;                                   (4.3)
```

or, using the shorthand assignment operator, we could use the equivalent statement

```
PTH |= 0x08;                                        (4.4)
```

Note that in Listing 4.1 we use the shorthand assignment operators `&=` and `|=` to first turn on segments *a*, *g*, and *d*, and then to turn them off. Try this program.

4.2 Example 4b – Turning a single bit on and off

Instead of having to figure out the hex value to AND and OR with PTH in order to turn on or off a particular bit we have written two assembly language routines that are called by the C function calls shown in Table 4.2. These assembly language routines are always available to you when you set up an *LBE_miniDRAGON_Plus2* stationery project. Listing 4.2 shows how you can modify the program in Listing 4.1 to produce the same result. Try it.

Table 4.2 C function calls for turning on or off a single bit of PTH

C Function Call	Meaning
`PTH_HI(int b);`	Sets bit *b* of PTH high
`PTH_LO(int b);`	Sets bit *b* of PTH low

Listing 4.2 Example 4b

```
// Example 4b: Single segments in 7-Segment Display
#include <hidef.h>              /* common defines and macros */
#include <mc9s12dg256.h>        /* derivative information */
#pragma LINK_INFO DERIVATIVE "mc9s12dg256b"

#include "main_asm.h"   /* interface to the assembly module */

void main(void) {
  PLL_init();          // set system clock frequency to 24 MHz
  seg7_enable();             // enable 7-segment display
  while(1){
    PTH_LO(0);               // turn on segment a
    ms_delay(500);           // half-second delay
    PTH_LO(6);               // turn on segment g
    ms_delay(500);           // half-second delay
    PTH_LO(3);               // turn on segment d
    ms_delay(500);           // half-second delay
    PTH_HI(0);               // turn off segment a
    ms_delay(500);           // half-second delay
    PTH_HI(6);               // turn off segment g
    ms_delay(500);           // half-second delay
    PTH_HI(3);               // turn off segment d
    ms_delay(500);           // half-second delay
  }
}
```

PROBLEMS

4.1 Modify Listing 4.2 to turn on segments *b*, *d*, *f* in sequence and then turn them off in the same sequence.

4.2 Modify Listing 4.2 to turn on segments *f*, *a*, *b* in sequence and then turn them off in the same sequence.

4.3 Modify Listing 4.2 to turn on segments *e*, *g*, *b* in sequence and then turn them off in the same sequence.

4.4 Modify Listing 4.2 to make a snake that turns on the following segments in sequence: *a*, *b*, *g*, *e*, *d*, *c*, *g*, *f*. Only one segment should be on at a time and the sequence should repeat endlessly.

4.5 Modify Listing 4.2 to make a snake that turns on the following segments in sequence: *a*, *f*, *g*, *c*, *d*, *e*, *g*, *b*. Only one segment should be on at a time and the sequence should repeat endlessly.

Example 5

Pushbutton Switches: S1 and S2

In this example we will show how to read the two pushbutton switches, S1 and S2, on the miniDRAGON-Plus2 board. We will first show you how to do this in C, and then we will provide new C function calls to do this.

5.1 Example 5a – Switches S1 and S2

Switches S1 and S2 on the miniDRAGON-Plus2 board are connected to bits 4 and 3 of Port AD0 as shown in Fig. 5.1. If the switches are not being pressed the 10 kΩ pullup resistors will cause the voltage at pins 4 and 3 to be 5 volts and therefore a read of PORTAD0 will read these two bits as 1. Closing a switch will cause the input to that bit of PORTAD0 to be grounded and therefore that bit will read 0 when PORTAD0 is read.

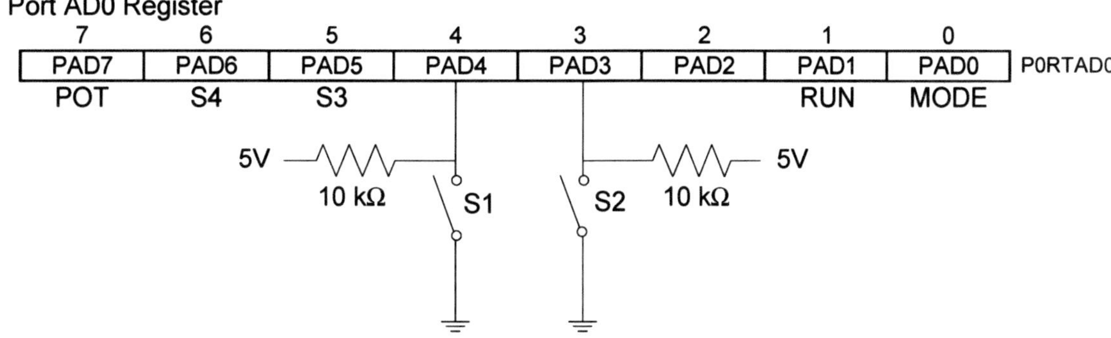

Figure 5.1 Switch connections to PORTAD0

To tell if switch S1 is being pressed we must first read the PORTAD0 register and then test to see if bit 4 is a 1 (S1 open) or 0 (S1 closed). We can do this by ANDing the value read from PORTAD0 with the mask 00010000 (0x10). If the switch is open (not being pressed) then the result of this AND operation will be 0x10. On the other hand, if the switch is closed (being pressed) then the result of this AND operation will be 0x00.

A C program that will display a 1 on the 7-segment display if switch S1 is being pressed and display a 2 on the 7-segment display if switch S2 is being pressed is shown in Listing 5.1. Note that the expression

```
(PORTAD0 & 0x10) == 0
```

will be true if bit 4 of PORTAD0 is 0, i.e., if switch S1 is being pressed. Similarly, the expression

```
(PORTAD0 & 0x08) == 0
```

will be true if bit 3 of PORTAD0 is 0, i.e., if switch S2 is being pressed.

The pins connected to PORTAD0 can also be used as input pins for the analog-to-digital (A/D) converter AD0 (see Example 11). There is also a second 8-channel A/D converter called AD1. To indicate that we want to use pins 3 and 4 of AD0 as digital inputs rather than analog inputs we must set bits 3 and 4 of register ATD0DIEN to 1. We do this in Listing 5.1 with the statement

```
ATD0DIEN = 0x18;          // enable S1 and S2
```

If you download the program in Listing 5.1 to the miniDRAGON-Plus2 board and press switch S1 then a 1 should be displayed on the 7-segment display. If you press switch S2 then a 2 should be displayed. What will be displayed if you press both switches at the same time? Try it.

Listing 5.1 Example 5a

```
// Example 5a: Pushbutton Switches
#include <hidef.h>              /* common defines and macros */
#include <mc9s12dg256.h>        /* derivative information */
#pragma LINK_INFO DERIVATIVE "mc9s12dg256b"

#include "main_asm.h"    /* interface to the assembly module */

void main(void) {
  PLL_init();         // set system clock frequency to 24 MHz
  seg7_enable();      // enable 7-segment display
  ATD0DIEN = 0x18;    // enable S1 and S2
  while(1){
      if((PORTAD0 & 0x10) == 0)
         seg7dec(1);
      else
         seg7_off();
      if((PORTAD0 & 0x08) == 0)
         seg7dec(2);
      else
         seg7_off();
  }
}
```

Note the use of the equality operator == in Listing 5.1. The C operators for equality and inequality are shown in Table 5.1.

Table 5.1 Equality and Inequality Operators

Operator	Description
==	Test for equality
!=	Test for inequality

5.2 Example 5b – Function calls for reading switches S1 and S2

Instead of having to remember which bit in which register switches S1 and S2 are connected to we have written assembly language routines that are called by the C function calls shown in Table 5.2. These assembly language routines are always available to you when you set up an *LBE_miniDRAGON_Plus2* stationery project. Listing 5.2 shows how you can modify the program in Listing 5.1 to produce the same result. Try it.

Table 5.2 C function calls for reading switches S1 and S2

C Function Call	Meaning
`SW12_enable();`	Enable switches S1 and S2
`SW1_down();`	Returns **true** if S1 is down
`SW2_down();`	Returns **true** if S2 is down
`SW1_up();`	Returns **true** if S1 is up
`SW2_up();`	Returns **true** if S2 is up

Listing 5.2 Example 5b

```
// Example 5b: Pushbutton Switches using C function calls
#include <hidef.h>              /* common defines and macros */
#include <mc9s12dg256.h>        /* derivative information */
#pragma LINK_INFO DERIVATIVE "mc9s12dg256b"

#include "main_asm.h"    /* interface to the assembly module */

void main(void) {
  PLL_init();         // set system clock frequency to 24 MHz
  seg7_enable();      // enable 7-segment display
  SW12_enable();      // enable S1 and S2
  while(1){
      if(SW1_down())
         seg7dec(1);
      else
         seg7_off();
      if(SW2_down())
         seg7dec(2);
      else
         seg7_off();
  }
}
```

PROBLEMS

5.1 Modify Listing 5.2 to turn on segment *a* when switch S1 is being pressed and turn on segment *d* when switch S2 is being pressed.

5.2 Modify Listing 5.2 so that pressing switch S1 will toggle a 1 on and off on the 7-segment display. That is, the first time S1 is pressed a 1 is displayed and stays displayed when S1 is released. The second time S1 is pressed, the display goes off. The third time S1 is pressed the 1 is displayed again.

5.3 Consider the program shown in Listing 5.3. What will happen when you press switch S1? What will happen when you press switch S2? What will happen when you press both switch S1 and S2 together? Try it.

Listing 5.3 Example 5c

```
// Example 5c: Pushbutton Switches - Problem 5.3
#include <hidef.h>              /* common defines and macros */
#include <mc9s12dg256.h>        /* derivative information */
#pragma LINK_INFO DERIVATIVE "mc9s12dg256b"

#include "main_asm.h"    /* interface to the assembly module */

void main(void) {
  PLL_init();          // set system clock frequency to 24 MHz
  seg7_enable();          // enable 7-segment display
  SW12_enable();          // enable S1 and S2
  while(1){
      while(SW1_down()){
         seg7dec(1);
      }
      seg7_off();
      while(SW2_down()){
         seg7dec(2);
      }
      seg7_off();
  }
}
```

Example 6

Hex Keypad

In this example we will show how to read values from a hex keypad connected to the keypad header J13 on the miniDRAGON-Plus2 board. We will first show how to do this entirely in C and will then provide new C function calls written in assembly language to make it easy to do this.

6.1 4 x 4 Hex Keypad

Consider a 4 x 4 keypad connected to Port A of a MC9S12DG256 as shown in Figure 6.1. The keypad header J13 on the miniDRAGON-Plus2 board is connected to Port A in this fashion. Pins *PA0–PA3* are configured as outputs and pins *PA4–PA7* are configured as inputs. These four inputs are pulled up to 5 volts with four pull-up resistors. The C statement `PUCR = 0x01;` will enable these pull-up resistors. Thus, if all the key switches are open the four bits *PA4–PA7* will all be read as 1's. If a zero is written to only one of the rows *PA0–PA3*, then a key in that row that is pressed will cause the input connected to its column to go low. This can be read by the MCU to determine which key has been pressed.

For example, suppose that *PA1* is brought low while *PA0*, *PA2*, and *PA3* are high. That is, a 1101, or $D, is written to the low nibble of Port A. If Port A is then read and the high nibble, *PA4–PA7*, is not $F, then either key 4, 5, 6, or B, must have been pressed. If *PA4* is low, i.e. Port A reads $ED, then key 4 was pressed. If *PA5* is low, i.e. Port A reads $DD, then key 5 was pressed. If *PA6* is low, i.e. Port A reads $BD, then key 6 was pressed. If *PA7* is low, i.e. Port A reads $7D, then key *B* was pressed. In a similar way we could determine the key codes for all 16 keys and store them in a table called *keycodes* as shown in Table 6.1.

The C function *key_scan()* given in Listing 6.1 reads each of the 16 codes in the table *keycodes*, stores the code in *PORTA*, and then reads back the contents of *PORTA*. The key value is found when the read back value is equal to the key code. Note that *key_scan()* returns a value of 16 if no key is being pressed.

The C function *get_key()* shown in Listing 6.2 will wait for a key to be pressed and return the hex value of the key pressed. Note that it does this by using the C *do-while* looping statement that will continue to loop as long as *key_scan()* returns a value of 16; i.e. as long as no key is being pressed.

Once you obtain a keypad value using the word *get_key()* you usually want to do something with this value such as display the hex digit on a liquid crystal display (LCD) that will be described in Example 7. If, for example, you want to display the value of the first key pressed at the current cursor position on an LCD and then display the value of the second key pressed at the next cursor position you could run into a problem. After displaying the first value, if your finger was still pressing the key, the program would display this same value at the next cursor position. In fact, the first digit would streak across the LCD display as long as you keep your finger down! You need to be able to wait until you have released your finger before waiting to press another key. The C function *wait_fo_keyup()* in Listing 6.2 will do this. The C program *main()* shown in Listing 6.3 will display any key you press on the 7-segment display of the miniDRAGON-Plus2.

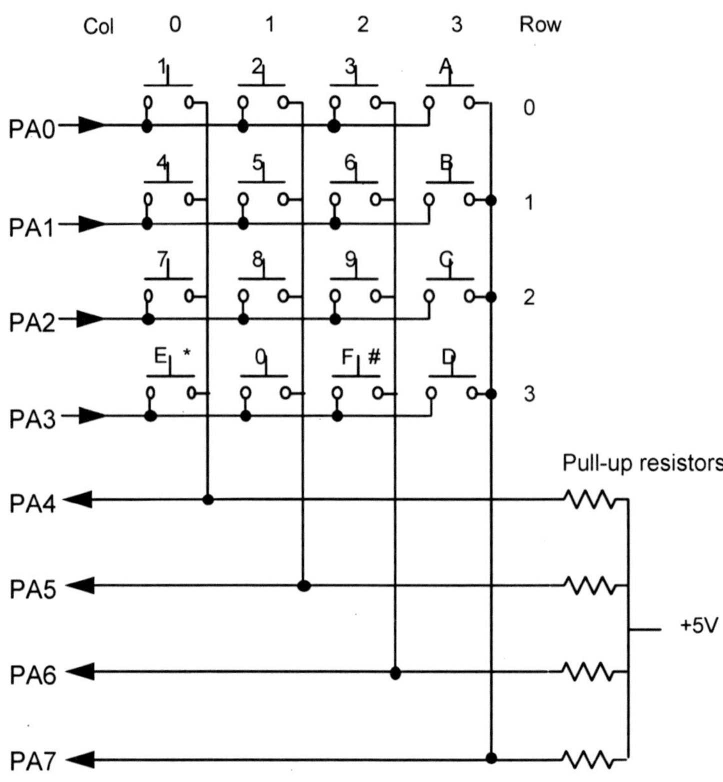

Figure 6.1 Connecting a 4 x 4 keypad to Port A

Table 6.1 Keycodes for 4 x 4 hex keypad

key	0	1	2	3	4	5	6	7	8	9	A	B	C	D	* E	# F
code	D7	EE	DE	BE	ED	DD	BD	EB	DB	BB	7E	7D	7B	77	E7	B7

Listing 6.1 C function *key_scan()*

```
int key_scan(void){
  const char keycodes[] = {
         0xD7,0xEE,0xDE,0xBE,
         0xED,0xDD,0xBD,0xEB,
         0xDB,0xBB,0x7E,0x7D,
         0x7B,0x77,0xE7,0xB7
  };
  int i,j, key;
  char readback;
  int found;
  i = 0;
  key = 16;                      // return 16 if no key pressed
  found = 0;
  while((i < 16) && (found == 0)){
    PORTA = keycodes[i];         // write keycode to PORTA
    for(j = 0; j<10; j++){
    }                            // wait a bit
    readback = PORTA;
    if(readback == keycodes[i]){ // read back PORTA, if same
      key  = i;                  //   get key number
      found = 1;                 //     and exit loop
    }
    else
      i++;                       // else check next key
  }
  return key;                    //    return key
}
```

Listing 6.2 C function *get_key()*

```
int get_key(void){
  int key;
  do {
    key = key_scan();
  }
  while(key == 16);
  return key;
}

void wait_for_keyup(void){
  while(key_scan() != 16){
  }
}
```

Listing 6.3 Example 6a

```
// Example 6a: 4 x 4 keypad in C
#include <hidef.h>            /* common defines and macros */
#include <mc9s12dg256.h>      /* derivative information */
#pragma LINK_INFO DERIVATIVE "mc9s12dg256b"

#include "main_asm.h"   /* interface to the assembly module */

int key_scan(void);
int get_key(void);
void wait_for_keyup(void);

void main(void) {
  int c;
  PLL_init();         // set system clock frequency to 24 MHz
  seg7_enable();      // enable 7-segment display
  DDRA = 0x0F;        // Port A: A7:A4 inputs, A3:A0 outputs
  PUCR = 0x01;        // enable pullup resistors
  while(1){
      c = get_key();
      seg7dec(c);
      wait_for_keyup();
  }
}
```

6.2 Keypad C Function Calls

Sometimes the switches making up a keypad will have a tendency to bounce when the are pressed. That is, when contact is first made it may open momentarily before closing for good. This could lead to thinking that the key was up (and therefore continuing the program) when it really wasn't. In such a situation a digit might inadvertently get displayed twice. To solve this problem key switches are debounced, either in hardware or software. The software solution is to delay for about 10 ms after a key pressing is sensed. If the key is read again and it is the same value as before, then you can conclude that the key has stopped bouncing and the correct value has been read.

We have written assembly language routines for reading the 4 x 4 keypad that include the debounce delays. (The assembly language routines to read pushbutton switches S1 and S1 described in Example 5 also include debounce delays.) The C function calls to access these routines are shown in Table 6.2. The *keypad_enable*() routine will properly set the data direction register and enable the pull-up resistors of Port A. An example of using these routines to display the key value pressed on the 7-segment display is shown in Listing 6.4. Try it.

Table 6.2 C function calls for reading a 4 x 4 keypad

C Function Call	Meaning
`keypad_enable();`	Enable the keypad
`int getkey();`	Waits to press key and returns value
`void wait_keyup();`	Waits until key is not being pressed
`int keyscan();`	Returns 16 if no key is being pressed Returns key value if key is being pressed

Listing 6.4 Example 6b

```
// Example 6b: 4 x 4 keypad using C function calls
#include <hidef.h>              /* common defines and macros */
#include <mc9s12dg256.h>        /* derivative information */
#pragma LINK_INFO DERIVATIVE "mc9s12dg256b"

#include "main_asm.h"    /* interface to the assembly module */

void main(void) {
char c;
  PLL_init();        // set system clock frequency to 24 MHz
  seg7_enable();     // enable 7-segment display
  keypad_enable();
  while(1){
      c = getkey();
      seg7dec(c);
      wait_keyup();
  }
}
```

Example 7

Liquid Crystal Displays

In this example we will show how to write characters to a liquid crystal display (LCD) connected to the LCD header on the miniDRAGON-Plus2 board. We will provide new C function calls to make it easy to do this. The example will assume you have a 16 x 2 LCD but the same function calls will work with a 20 x 4 LCD.

7.1 Liquid Crystal Displays

A liquid crystal display (LCD) is a common type of display used in a variety of applications such as watches, calculators, and laptop computers. Its big advantage is that it uses much less power than an LED and therefore can be used in battery-powered applications. An LCD consists of a liquid crystal material sandwiched between two conducting plates. An AC voltage applied between the two conductors will cause the reflectance (or transmittance) of the liquid crystal to change making a character visible. LCD displays come in a variety of configurations.

For example, the Sanyo DM1623 displays 2 lines of 16 characters. This display and many other common ones use a built-in Hitachi HD44780 LCD Controller/Driver that performs all of the functions needed to drive the LCD and provides an easy interface to a microcontroller using an 8-bit data bus, *DB0-DB7*, and three control signals, *RS*, *R/W*, and *E*. It is also possible to communicate with the Hitachi HD44780 LCD Controller/Driver over a 4-bit data bus. This is what the miniDRAGON-Plus2 does. The relationships between *RS*, *R/W*, and *E* are shown in Figure 7.1.

RS	R/W	E	Operation
0	0		Write instruction code
0	1		Read busy flag and address counter
1	0		Write data
1	1		Read data

Figure 7.1 Relationships between RS, R/W, and E

The signal, *RS*, can be thought of as a register select signal that selects either the LCD control register (*RS* = 0) or the LCD data register (*RS* = 1). The read/write signal *R/W* is 1 for a read operation and 0 for a write operation. Data or instruction codes are written on the falling edge of *E*, and *E* must be high for a read operation.

The HD44780 has its own instruction set shown in Table 7.1. (For a complete data sheet go to *http://www.hitachi.com/*.) The first eight are instruction codes that are written to the LCD control register with *RS* = 0 and *R/W* = 0 as shown in Figure 7.1. The last entry in Table 7.1 shows the format of the busy flag and address counter when reading from the LCD control register with *RS* = 0 and *R/W* = 1 as shown in Figure 7.1.

Table 7.1 HD44780 Instruction Set

Instruction	DB7	DB6	DB5	DB4	DB3	DB2	DB1	DB0	Description
Clear display	0	0	0	0	0	0	0	1	Clears display & returns cursor to home. Sets I/D=1 in Entry Mode.
Return home	0	0	0	0	0	0	1	x	Returns cursor to home position (Address 0) Set DD RAM address to zero.
Entry mode set	0	0	0	0	0	1	I/D	S	I/D=1: increment cursor; S=0: normal ; I/D=0: decrement cursor; S=1 shift display.
Display ON/OFF control	0	0	0	0	1	D	C	B	Sets ON/OFF all display (D), cursor (C), and blink of cursor (B).
Cursor or display shift	0	0	0	1	S/C	R/L	x	x	S/C=1: display shift; S/C=0: cursor move; R/L=1: shift right; R/L=0: shift left.
Function set	0	0	1	DL	N	F	x	x	DL=1: 8 bits; DL=0: 4 bits; N=1: 2 line; N=0: 1 line; F=1: 5x10 dots; F=0; 5x7 dots.
Set the CG RAM address	0	1	CG RAM address						Sets the CG RAM address, after which CG RAM data is sent and received.
Set the DD RAM address	1	DD RAM address							Sets the DD RAM address, after which DD RAM data is sent and received.
Read busy flag & address	BF	Address counter							Read busy flag (BF) and address counter contents.

The HD44780 contains a 128-byte data display memory (DD RAM) that contains the ASCII codes of the characters being displayed on the LCD display. This DD RAM address is set (address 0 is the display home position) using the *Set the DD RAM address* instruction. After this is done, subsequent data writes will write the ASCII code of the character to be displayed to the DD RAM address (and display the character) and then increment the DD RAM address so that the next character will be displayed in the next location.

The HD44780 also contains a 64-byte character-generator memory (CG RAM) that can be used to change the font of up to 16 different characters. If you are interested in doing this you can consult an HD44780 data sheet.

The data bus *DB0-DB7* on the HD44780 can be connected directly to a microcontroller's data bus and the controller can be wired up to respond to reads and writes to a particular series of addresses. The HD44780 can also be connected to the parallel I/O ports on a microcontroller and then software can be written to produce the control signals shown in Figure 7.1. This is the approach taken on the miniDRAGON-Plus2 board.

The diagram in Figure 7.2 shows how the LCD connector on the miniDRAGON-Plus2 board is connected to Port K of the MC68HCS912DG256. Note than only the upper 4 bits of the LCD controller are connected to *PTK*[5:2] while the enable signal *E* is connected to *PK1* and the register select signal *RS* is connected to *PK0*. The read/write line is connected ground on the DRAGON12-Plus board providing write-only operation of the LCD display. In this case you will not be able to read the busy flag. This is not a disadvantage because reading this flag is often problematic and an alternative is to simply delay after writing to the LCD. This is what we will do.

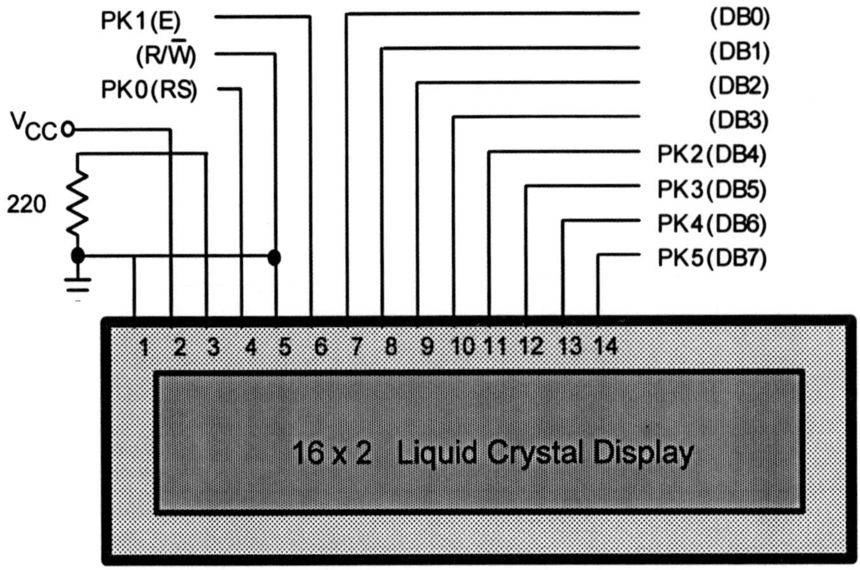

Figure 7.2 Interfacing to a Liquid Crystal Display on the miniDRAGON-Plus2 board

Before you can write to the LCD you must initialize it. We have provided the C function call *LCD_init()* to do this. This function initializes it for 4-bit, 2 line, 5 x 7 dot operation, display on, cursor off, no blinking, then clears the display and sets the cursor to the home position.

You can set the cursor to any position on the display by calling the built-in C function call *set_lcd_addr(char ad)* where *ad* is an 8-bit hex address whose display position is shown in Fig. 7.3. Note that there is a gap between the end of the first line and the beginning of the second line. If you are using a 20 x 4 LCD the hex address of the first character of line 3 is 0x14 (which is a continuation of line 1) and the hex address of the first character of line 4 is 0x54 (which is a continuation of line 2).

00	01	02	03	04	05	06	07	08	09	0A	0B	0C	0D	0E	0F
40	41	42	43	44	45	46	47	48	49	4A	4B	4C	4D	4E	4F

Figure 7.3 Hex addresses of 16 x 2 LCD display

A list of all the C function calls that we have provided assembly language routines for are shown in Table 7.2. Listing 7.1 shows how to display a message on each line of the display. Try it.

Table 7.2 C Function calls for LCD display

Function	Description
`void lcd_init(void);`	Initialize LCD display (clears display)
`void set_lcd_addr(char);`	Set cursor address (see Fig. 7.3)
`void data8(char);`	Write ASCII character to display at cursor location
`void instr8(char);`	Write instruction to display (see Table 7.1)
`void clear_lcd(void);`	Clear LCD display
`void hex2lcd(char);`	Write hex digit (0 – F) to LCD display
`char hex2asc(char);`	Convert hex digit (0 – F) to ASCII code
`void type_lcd(char*);`	Display ASCIIZ string on LCD display at cursor location

Listing 7.1 Example 7

```
// Example 7: LCD Display
#include <hidef.h>           /* common defines and macros */
#include <mc9s12dg256.h>     /* derivative information */
#pragma LINK_INFO DERIVATIVE "mc9s12dg256b"

#include "main_asm.h"   /* interface to the assembly module */

void main(void) {
  char* q1;
  char* q2;
  q1 = "miniDRAGON-Plus2";
  q2 = "is FUN";
  PLL_init();       // set system clock frequency to 24 MHz

  lcd_init();               // enable lcd
  set_lcd_addr(0x00);
  type_lcd(q1);             // write q1
  set_lcd_addr(0x45);
  type_lcd(q2);             // write q2
  for(;;){
  }                         // wait forever
}
```

The function *data8(char)* in Table 7.2 will display the character whose ASCII code is passed as a parameter. The ASCII codes of all characters are shown in Table 7.3. In this table the upper nibble of the ASCII code is given by the column heading and the lower nibble is given by the row number. For example, the hex ASCII code for upper-case *A* is 0x41 and the ASCII code for lower-case *k* is 0x6B. Thus, the function call *data8(0x41)* will display an upper-case *A* at the current cursor position. The cursor is automatically incremented when this function is called.

The function *hex2lcd(char)* in Table 7.2 will display the hex digit passed as the parameter on the LCD display. For example, *hex2lcd(0xA)* will display the *A* on the LCD display by first converting 0xA to the ASCII code 0x41 using the built-in function *hex2asc(char)*. The cursor is automatically incremented when this function is called.

Table 7.3 Standard ASCII Codes

Dec	→	0	16	32	48	64	80	96	112
↓	Hex	0	1	2	3	4	5	6	7
0	0	NUL	DLE	Blank	0	@	P		p
1	1	SOH	DC1	!	1	A	Q	a	q
2	2	STX	DC2	“	2	B	R	b	r
3	3	ETX	DC3	#	3	C	S	c	s
4	4	EOT	DC4	$	4	D	T	d	t
5	5	ENQ	NAK	%	5	E	U	e	u
6	6	ACK	SYN	&	6	F	V	f	v
7	7	BEL	ETB	‘	7	G	W	g	w
8	8	BS	CAN	(	8	H	X	h	x
9	9	HT	EM	)	9	I	Y	i	y
10	A	LF	SUB	*	:	J	Z	j	z
11	B	VT	ESC	+	;	K	[	k	{
12	C	FF	FS	,	<	L	\	l	|
13	D	CR	GS	-	=	M	]	m	}
14	E	SO	RS	.	>	N	^	n	~
15	F	SI	US	/	?	O	_	o	DEL

PROBLEMS

7.1 Modify Listing 7.1 to display your name centered on the first two rows.

7.2 Modify Listing 7.1 to display the digits 0 – 9 in a row using a *for* loop.

7.3 Modify Listing 7.1 to display the following figure made of $ signs centered on the display.

```
$$$$$$
$    $
```

Example 8

Serial Communication Interface (SCI)

In this example we will show how to communicate from the COM1 serial port on your PC to the SCI port on the miniDRAGON-Plus2 board. We will provide new C function calls to make it easy to do this.

8.1 Asynchronous Serial I/O

There are two basic types of serial communication: *synchronous* and *asynchronous*. In synchronous communication the timing is controlled by a standard clock at both the transmitter and receiver ends, and data are normally sent in blocks that often contain error checking. On the other hand the timing for asynchronous communication is handled one character at a time and while the clocks at the transmitter and receiver must be approximately the same, they are resynchronized with each character. Because each character requires these additional synchronizing bits, asynchronous communication is slower than synchronous communication. However, it is simpler to implement and is in widespread use.

Asynchronous serial communication uses a *start bit* to tell when a particular character is being sent. This is illustrated in Figure 8.1 which shows the transmitted waveform when the character *"T"* (ASCII code = 0x54) is sent with odd parity. Before a character is sent the line is in the high, or *mark* state. The line is then brought low (called a *space*) and held low for a time τ called the bit time. This first space is called the *start bit*. It is typically followed by seven or eight data bits. The least significant bit *D0* is transmitted first. For example, in Figure 8.1 the seven bits corresponding to the ASCII code 0x54 (the character *"T"*) are sent starting with *D0*. These seven bits are followed by a *parity bit*. This bit is set to a 1 or a 0 such that the sum of the number of 1's transmitted is either even or odd. We have used odd parity in Figure 8.1. Since three 1's were sent (*D2*, *D4*, and *D6*) the parity bit is zero. Often a character is sent with no parity and 8 data bits. The parity bit is followed by one or two stop bits which are always high (a *mark*). The next character will be indicated by the presence of the next start bit.

The reciprocal of the bit time is called the *baud rate*. Some common baud rates used in serial communication are given in Table 8.1. We will provide you with a C function call that allows you to set any baud rate when you initialize the SCI port .

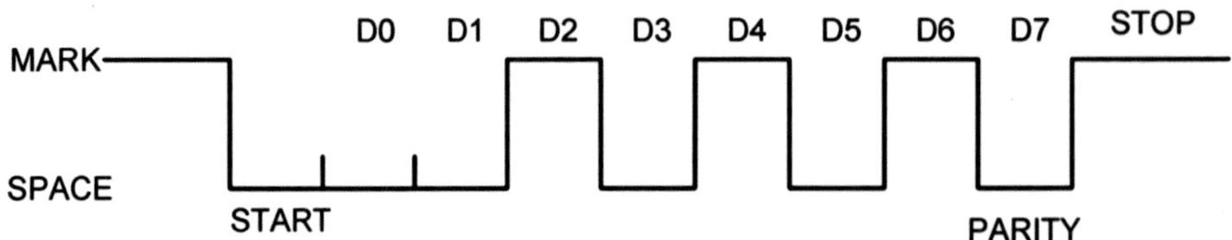

Fig. 8.1 ASCII code 54H = 1010100 ("T") sent with odd parity

Table 8.1
Common Asynchronous Serial Baud Rates

Baud rate	Bit time (msec)	No. of STOP bits	Char. time (msec.)	Char./sec.
110	9.09	2	100.00	10
300	3.33	1	33.3 3	30
600	1.67	1	16.67	60
1200	0.833	1	8.33	120
2400	0.417	1	4.17	240
4800	0.208	1	2.08	480
9600	0.104	1	1.04	960
14400	0.069	1	0.69	1440
19200	0.052	1	0.52	1920
28800	0.035	1	0.35	2880
38400	0.026	1	0.26	3840

8.2 The 68HCS12 SCI Interface

The MC68HC9S12GP256 has two separate SCI modules, SCI0 and SCI1. On the miniDRAGON-Plus2 board SCI0 is connected to the P1 connector that you use to connect to the serial port of the PC when you program your board. The second module SCI1 is connected to the P2 connector.

A functional block diagram of the serial communication interface is shown in Figure 8.2. The main function of the SCI is to transform parallel data from the HCS12 into serial data and send it out through the transmit data pin *TxD*, and to receive serial data through the receive data pin *RxD* and transform it to parallel data that can be read by the HCS12.

The signals *TxD* (pins *PS1* or *PS3*) and *RxD* (pins *PS0* or *PS2*) are generally connected to a 9-pin "D" connector through an EIA-232-D (formally RS-232C) driver/receiver chip. This driver/receiver transforms the logic 0 (0 volts) and logic 1 (5 volts) signals to +12 volts and –12 volts respectively. (Sometimes +5 volts and –5 volts are used.) This allows for more noise immunity when sending the signals over a long distance. Pin 2 on the "D" connector is normally the "transmit" pin *TxD* on the microcontroller board and pin 3 is the "receive" pin *RxD*. But if a straight-through cable is connected from the serial port on a PC to your target HCS12 board then the PC's "transmit" pin must be pin 3 so that it is connected to the *RxD* pin on the HCS12 board. Similarly, pin 2 on the PC will be the "receive" pin so that it is connected to the *TxD* pin on the HCS12 board.

If you want to communicate between two miniDRAGON-Plus2 boards using the SCI port it is necessary to interchange the wires in the cable so that pin 2 at one end is connected to pin 3 at the other end and vice versa. We call this a *null modem.*

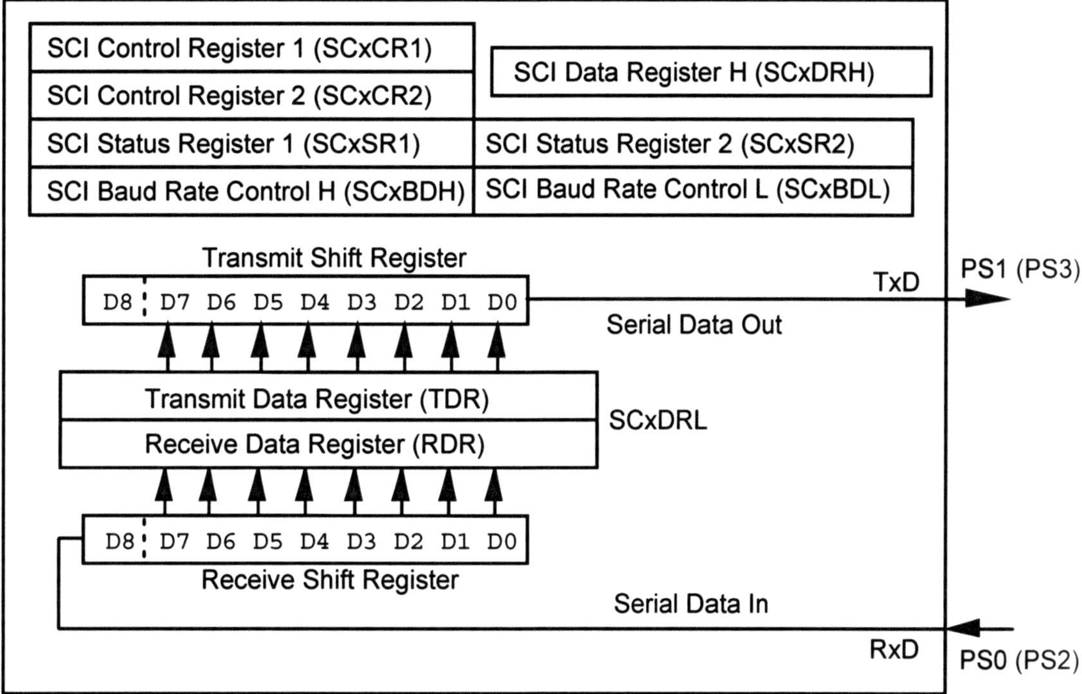

Fig. 8.2 Functional diagram of the Serial Communications Interface (SCI)

To use the SCI ports on the HCS12 it is necessary to program a number of different registers, some of which are shown in Fig. 8.2. We have done this for you by providing the C function calls shown in Table 8.2.

Table 8.2 C Function calls for the SCI port

Function	Description
`void SCI0_init(int b);`	Initialize SCI0 with baud rate *b*
`char inchar0(void);`	Wait for character in SCI0 and return char
`void outchar0(char c);`	Output character *c* out SCI0 TxD pin
`void SCI1_init(int b);`	Initialize SCI1 with baud rate *b*
`char inchar1(void);`	Wait for character in SCI1 and return char
`void outchar1(char c);`	Output character *c* out SCI1 TxD pin

Listing 8.1 is a program that initializes the SCI0 port to 9600 baud, waits for a character to come in *RxD*, and then sends the same character back out *TxD*. To test this program download it to the miniDRAGON-Plus2 board in the usual way, execute the program, and then make sure that you close the Real-Time Debugger window. Then run any convenient terminal program running at 9600 baud. (A simple terminal program

called *host.exe* that will work can be downloaded from www.lbebooks.com.) Pressing any key on the PC keyboard will send the ASCII code of the key out the serial port to the miniDRAGON-Plus2 which will echo it back to the PC where it will be displayed. Note that the terminal program does not display a character on the screen until it has made a round trip to the miniDRAGON-Plus2 board and back. Try it.

Listing 8.1 Example 8a

```
// Example 8a: SCI Echo
#include <hidef.h>              /* common defines and macros */
#include <mc9s12dg256.h>        /* derivative information */
#pragma LINK_INFO DERIVATIVE "mc9s12dg256b"

#include "main_asm.h"   /* interface to the assembly module */

void main(void) {
char c;
   PLL_init();          // set system clock frequency to 24 MHz
   SCI0_init(9600);     // initialize SCI0 at 9600 baud
   while(1){
      c = inchar0();        // wait for character
      outchar0(c);          // echo it back
   }
}
```

In Listing 8.2 we have modified Listing 8.1 by having the character typed on the keyboard displayed on the LCD display as well as echoed back to the PC. If you are using a 16 x 2 LCD note that when you get to the end of the first line of the LCD display you must type 24 characters before a character gets displayed on the second line. (Recall the LCD memory addresses in Fig. 7.3.)

Listing 8.2 Example 8b

```
// Example 8b: SCI Echo with LCD display
#include <hidef.h>       /* common defines and macros */
#include <mc9s12dg256.h>      /* derivative information */
#pragma LINK_INFO DERIVATIVE "mc9s12dg256b"

#include "main_asm.h" /* interface to the assembly module */

void main(void) {
char c;
   PLL_init();          // set system clock frequency to 24 MHz
   lcd_init();          // enable lcd
   SCI0_init(9600);     // initialize SCI0 at 9600 baud
   while(1){
     c = inchar0();     // wait for character
     data8(c);          // write it to the LCD
     outchar0(c);       // echo it back
   }
}
```

PROBLEMS

8.1 Modify Listing 8.2 to type your name on the PC keyboard and display it on the second row of the LCD display as you type it.

8.2 Write a program that uses the hex keypad described in Exercise 6. As you type characters on the keyboard, convert the hex value to ASCII and send the character out the SCI0 port. Test the program by running a terminal program on the PC that should display the characters that you type on the keypad.

Example 9

Binary to ASCII String Conversion

In this example we will show how a binary number can be converted to an ASCII string that can be displayed on an LCD display or PC screen.

9.1 Binary Number to ASCII String Conversion

To display the value of a 16-bit interger (*int*) or a 32-bit long integer (*long*) on a computer screen or LCD display it is first necessary to convert this integer to a string of ASCII characters. The steps used to create this string of ASCII characters are illustrated in Figure 9.1. Note that the algorithm consists of dividing the number by the base and converting the remainder to an ASCII character.

Figure 9.2 shows the algorithm for a routine called *sharps* which will convert a 32-bit double number to an ASCII string according to the steps in Figure 9.1. Note that the index *pad* starts at the end of the buffer, buff, and gets decremented before storing each ASCII code in the buffer. When the entire double number has been converted buff[pad] will contain the first ASCII character in the number string.

We have written assembly language routines called *sharp*, *sharps*, and *ddiv* to implement this algorithm and have included them in the *main.asm* file. We call the routine *sharp* in the two C function calls *write_int_lcd(int)* and *write_long_lcd(long)* shown in Table 9.1. The function *write_int_lcd(int)* will display a 16-bit integer right-justified in a field of 5 digits. The function *write_long_lcd(long)* will display a 32-bit long integer right-justified in a field of 10 digits. Listing 9.1 shows an example of using these functions. Try it.

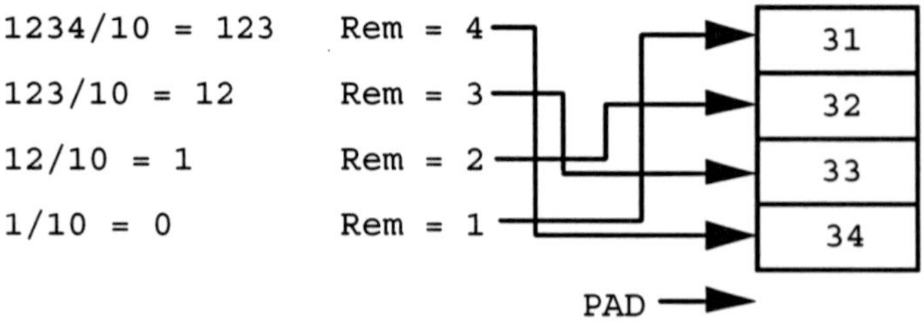

Figure 9.1 Steps for creating an ASCII number string

SHARPS: convert the double number *val32* to an ASCII string in a given *base*. The digits are converted least significant digit first and stored in memory starting at the end of the string. If the base is 16 then 0x37 must be added to the remainder to obtain the ASCII codes for A – F.

```
void sharps(long val32, int base) {
        unsigned char c;
        int rem;
        long quot;
        int pad;
        unsigned char buff[12];
        pad = 12;
        do{
          quot = val32/base;
          rem = val32 % base;
          if(rem > 9){
            rem = rem + 7;
          }
          c = 0x30 + rem;
          pad--;
          buff[pad] = c;
          val32 = quot;
        } while(quot != 0);
}
```

Figure 9.2 Algorithms to convert a double number to an ASCII string

Listing 9.1 Example 9

```
// Example 9: Writing INTs and LONGs to LCD
#include <hidef.h>      /* common defines and macros */
#include <mc9s12dg256.h>     /* derivative information */
#pragma LINK_INFO DERIVATIVE "mc9s12dg256b"

#include "main_asm.h" /* interface to the assembly module */

int val16;
long val32;

void main(void) {
  PLL_init();       // set system clock frequency to 24 MHz
  lcd_init();                     // enable lcd
  val16 = 54321;
  set_lcd_addr(0x0);              // display 5-digit int
  write_int_lcd(val16);
  val32 = 2345678123;
  set_lcd_addr(0x40);             // display 10-digit long
  write_long_lcd(val32);
  while(1) {
  }
}
```

Table 9.1 C function calls for writing integers to the LCD

C Function Call	Meaning
`void write_int_lcd(int);`	Display a 16-bit integer right-justified in a field of 5 digits
`void write_long_lcd(long);`	Display a 32-bit integer right-justified in a field of 10 digits

PROBLEMS

9.1 Modify Listing 9.1 to display the 16-bit integer 123 in the center of the second row of the LCD display. Remember that *write_int_lcd(int)* will display leading blanks in a field of 5.

9.2 Modify Listing 9.1 to display the 32-bit long integer 1234567 in the center of the first row of the LCD display. Remember that *write_long_lcd(long)* will display leading blanks in a field of 10.

9.3 The algorithm shown in Fig. 9.2 will work for any base. If you want to display hex values on the LCD you can open the file *main.asm* and change the statement

```
bas10:  equ  10
```

on line 72 to

```
bas10:  equ  16
```

Then if you re-compile and re-run the program shown in Listing 9.1 the value 54321 will be displayed as its hex equivalent D431 and the value 2345678123 will be displayed as its hex equivalent 8BD0352B. Try it. Don't forget to change the value of *bas10* back to 10.

Example 10

ASCII String to Binary Conversion

In this example we will show how an ASCII number string can be converted to a binary number and use it to enter binary numbers from a keyboard or keypad. As an example we will design a simple calculator.

10.1 ASCII Number String to Binary Conversion

When you enter a number (such as 34671) from the keyboard the characters in the number are stored in a buffer as an ASCII string. If you were to type such a number on a hex keypad of the type we described in Example 6 then you could form an ASCII string by first converting each digit to an ASCII value using the function *hex2asc(char)* (see Example 7). If we want to store the *value* of this number as an integer or long integer variable we must convert the ASCII number string to a binary number. After performing some calculation it will be necessary to convert the binary number to an ASCII number string before the result can be displayed on the LCD display as shown in Example 9.

The decimal value 34671 can be represented as

$$\begin{aligned} 34671 &= 3\times10^4 + 4\times10^3 + 6\times10^2 + 7\times10 + 1 \\ &= 1 + 10\left(7 + 10\left(6 + 10\left(4 + 10(3)\right)\right)\right) \end{aligned} \qquad (10.1)$$

This form of representing a number can be used to convert an ASCII number string to a binary number using the algorithm *number* shown in Fig. 10.1.

```
long number(char*):
        char c;
        long dnum;
        dnum = 0;
        while(1){
          c = get_next_digit();
          if(digit_valid())
            dnum = dnum*base + c;
          else
            break;
        }
        return dnum;
```

Figure 10.1 Algorithm to convert an ASCII string to a double number

We have implemented this algorithm in assembly language, which you can call using the C function call shown in Table 10.1. In your C program you will have an ASCII number string stored in an array pointed to by the pointer *ptr*. This ASCII number string will be terminated by some character other than the ASCII codes for 0 – 9 (0x30 - 0x39). The algorithm continues to convert the ASCII string to a long integer as long as valid digits are in the string. It terminates with the first invalid digit. Thus, if you call *number(ptr)* it will return a long integer (32 bits) whose value is equal to the ASCII number string.

Table 10.1 C Function call for converting ASCII number string to binary

Function	Description
`long number(char* ptr);`	Return 32-bit binary number equal to ASCII number string

As an example of using this conversion routine we will write a C program for a simple calculator as shown in Listings 10.1. Note in Listing 10.1a we define a character array called *kbuf* that contains room for 12 characters. A 32-bit integer can have a maximum of 10 decimal digits (largest unsigned value is 4,294,967,295). We must leave space for a terminating invalid character and we might want to include a negative sign, so we will reserve 12 bytes for *kbuf*. We define a pointer called *ptr* to this keypad buffer using the statement

```
char* ptr;
```

and then set this pointer to the address of the first character in *kbuf* using the statement

```
ptr = kbuf;
```

Listing 10.1a Example 10

```
// Example 10: Calculator with ASCII string to number conversion
#include <hidef.h>       /* common defines and macros */
#include <mc9s12dg256.h>      /* derivative information */
#pragma LINK_INFO DERIVATIVE "mc9s12dg256b"

#include "main_asm.h" /* interface to the assembly module */

void main(void) {
  long op1, op2;                  // 32-bit operands
  char* ptr;                      // pointer to keypad buffer
  char* blanks;
  char  kbuf[12];                 // keypad buffer
  char  c, a;
  int  i;
  ptr = kbuf;
  blanks = "              ";
```

The remainder of the calculator program is shown in Listing 10.1b. After initializing the LCD and enabling the keypad we enter an infinite *while* loop.

Listing 10.1b Example 10 (cont.)

```
// Example 10: (cont.)
  PLL_init();                // set system clock frequency to 24 MHz
  lcd_init();                // enable lcd
  keypad_enable();           // enable keypad
  set_lcd_addr(0x00);        // display on 1st line
  i = 0;                     // kbuf index = 0
  while(1) {
    c = getkey();            // read keypad
    a = hex2asc(c);          // convert to ascii
    kbuf[i] = a;             //   and store in kbuf
    if(c < 10){              // if 0 - 9
      data8(a);              //   display on LCD
      wait_keyup();          //   wait to release key
      i++;                   // inc index
    } else {
      switch(c){
        case 0xE:            // if enter (*) key
          op1 = number(ptr);       // convert to binary
          set_lcd_addr(0x40);      // display on 2nd line
          write_long_lcd(op1);
          set_lcd_addr(0x00);      // clear 1st line
          type_lcd(blanks);
          wait_keyup();            // wait to release key
          i = 0;                   // reset kbuf index
          set_lcd_addr(0x00);      // display on 1st line
          break;
        case 0xA:            // if key A
          op2 = number(ptr);       // convert to binary
          op1 = op1 + op2;         // compute sum
          set_lcd_addr(0x40);      // display on 2nd line
          write_long_lcd(op1);
          set_lcd_addr(0x00);      // clear 1st line
          type_lcd(blanks);
          wait_keyup();            // wait to release key
          i = 0;                   // reset kbuf index
          set_lcd_addr(0x00);      // display on 1st line
          break;
        case 0xF:            // if clear (#) key
          clear_lcd();             // clear lcd display
          wait_keyup();            // wait to release key
          i = 0;                   // reset kbuf index
          break;
        default:
          break;
      }
    }
  }
}
```

We first wait for a key on the keypad to be pressed (using *getkey()*)and then return the value in *c*. This hex value is converted to ASCII using *hex2asc()* and the result (in *a*) is stored at the next location in *kbuf*. If the hex value *c* read from the keypad was less than 10 (i.e. 0 – 9) then it is displayed on the LCD using *data8(a)* and the program waits for you to lift your finger from the keypad. The *kbuf* index *i* is then incremented and you can continue to type in additional digits that will be displayed on the LCD and the ASCII values stored in *kbuf*.

If you type a key other than 0 – 9 (i.e. A – F) then the *else* part of the *if* statement will be executed. This contains the C *switch* statement which behaves like a *case* statement that executes one of several possible cases depending on the value of the *switch* expression, in this case the value of the hex value *c*. Note that the last statement in each of the cases is a *break* statement that terminates the *switch* statement.

If *c* is equal to 0xE (i.e. you pressed the E or * key) then the first case is executed. The first statement in this case is

```
op1 = number(ptr);
```

which will convert the ASCII string that you typed from the keypad to the long integer *op1*. Note that the ASCII value for E (0x45) was stored in *kbuf* when you pressed *E* and became the invalid digit that wasn't between 0 and 9. The next two statements will write this long integer right-justified in a field of 10 on the second line. The following two statements will clear the first line. After waiting for you to lift your finger the program then resets the *kbuf* index *i* to zero, sets the LCD address to the beginning of the first line, and then executes a *break* statement that will break out of the *switch* statement.

After typing in one number and entering it by pressing *E*, you can type in another number, but instead of pressing *E* you should press *A* this time, which will add the two numbers together and display the sum.

The second case in the *switch* statement will execute if you press the *A* key. It begins by displaying *op1* again on line two. The first statement will convert the second number you typed to binary and store the result in *op2*. Then the sum of *op1* and *op2* is stored back in *op1* and displayed on the second line. The first line is erased by overwriting it with blanks and then the program waits for you to lift your finger.

The LCD address is reset to the beginning of the first line and you can now enter another number. If you press *A* again the old sum will be added to your third number and the new sum will be displayed on the second line. You can continue to add numbers in this fashion. Pressing the F (or #) key will clear the display. Try it.

PROBLEMS

10.1 Modify Listing 10.1 to

a) display the result of subtracting the second number from the first number when you press the B key.
b) display the result of multiplying two numbers when you press the C key.
c) display the result of dividing the second number into the first number when you press the D key.

Example 11

Analog-to-Digital Converter

In this example we will show how to use the two 8-channel analog-to-digital (A/D) converters that are part of the MC9S12DG256 microcontroller.

11.1 Analog-to-Digital Conversion

A/D converters transform an analog voltage within a given voltage range into a corresponding digital number. For example, you might convert a voltage between 0 and 5 volts to an 8-bit binary number between 00000000 and 11111111. This represents a decimal number between 0 and 255. In this case, a change in the least-significant bit (LSB) of 1 corresponds to a change in voltage of 5V/256 = 19.5 mV. This quantization error, or step size, is inherent in any type of A/D conversion. We can minimize this error by using more bits. For example, a 10-bit A/D converter will have a step size between 0 and 5 volts of $5V/2^{10}$ = 5V/1024 = 4.9 mV. The MC9S12DG256 A/D converters can be programmed to do either 8-bit or 10-bit conversions. We will provide C functions to do 10-bit A/D conversions.

There are a number of different methods used for performing A/D conversions. One of the most popular, and the one used in the HCS12 microcontrollers, is the method of successive approximation. We will illustrate this method by using a 4-bit conversion in which the step size between 0 and 5 volts will be $5V/2^4$ = 5V/16 = 0.3125 V. For *n* bits the method of successive approximation requires *n* steps. The method is essentially a binary search as shown in Fig. 11.1 for four bits.

Suppose that the input analog voltage to convert is V_{in} = 3.5V. The first step is to guess the mid-range voltage of 2.5V corresponding to the binary number 1000. That is, we just set the most-significant bit. If this voltage (2.5V) is less than the voltage V_{in}, then we want to keep this bit, because we know the input voltage is greater than 2.5V. We then add the next most-significant bit and try 1100, or 3.75V, in step 2. This voltage is greater than 3.5V so we have overshot the mark and must discard this bit. Setting the next bit means that we will try the value 1010, or 3.125V is step 3. This value is less than 3.5V so we will keep this bit. Finally, we will set the last (least-significant) bit and try 1011, or 3.4375V in step 4. This is still less than 3.5V so we keep this bit. We are now done and our converted value is 1011 which really represents 3.4375V, but is within our error margin of 0.3125V.

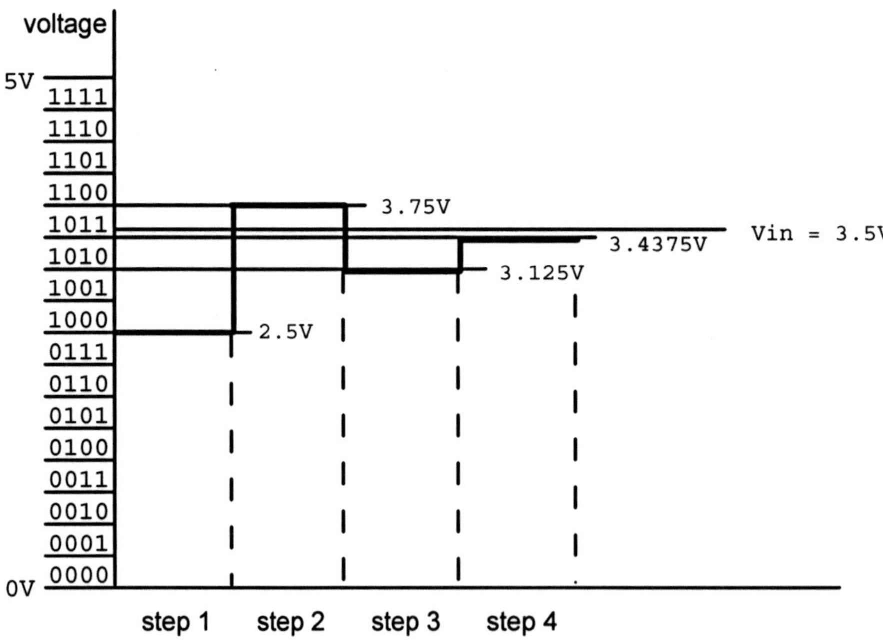

Figure 11.1 Illustrating the method of successive approximation

The successive approximation method illustrated in Fig. 11.1 can be implemented using a comparator and D/A converter as shown in Figure 11.2. Assuming a 4-bit A/D converter as shown in Figure 11.1, the control circuit will first put out the binary value 1000. The D/A converter will convert this value to V_{DA} = 2.5V. Because this value is less than V_{in} = 3.5V, the output, *C*, of the comparator will be 1. This tells the control circuit to keep this bit and output the value 1100 in the second step, as shown in Fig. 11.1. This time the value of V_{DA} = 3.75V is greater than V_{in} = 3.5V, and therefore the output, *C*, of the comparator will be 0. This tells the control circuit to throw away this bit and to output the value 1010 in step 3. This bit is kept as is the last bit as shown in Figure 11.1.

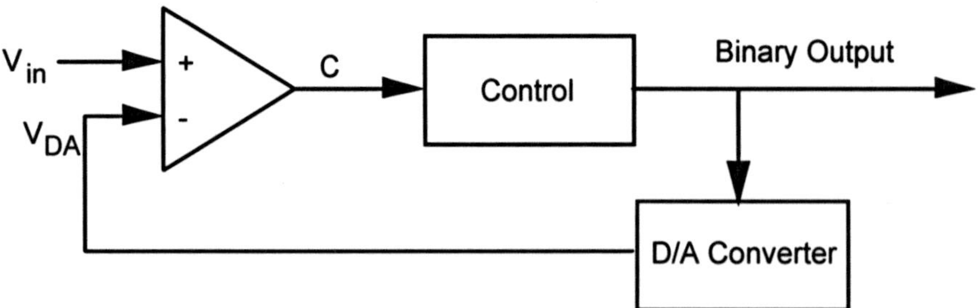

Figure 11.2 Implementing the method of successive approximation

11.2 Using the MC9S12DG256 A/D Converters

The MC9S12DG256 microcontroller has two 8-channel A/D converters, called ATD0 and ATD1, that can produce either 8-bit or 10-bit conversions. These A/D converters share the same input pins as PORTAD0 and PORTAD1, which can be used for digital inputs when the A/D converter is not being used. Pin 7 of PORTAD0 is connected to the center tap of the potentiometer on the miniDRAGON-Plus2 board. This input will vary between 0 and 5 volts as the white cap of the potentiometer (pot) is turned with a small screw driver. We will use this input to illustrate the use of ATD0.

There are lots of registers associated with the use of the A/D converters. To make it easy we have written several assembly language routines that are called by the C functions shown in Table 11.1. Listing 11.1 shows a program that reads channel 7 of ATD0, divides the value by 2 (to reduce noise in the least-significant bit), and displays the result on the LCD display. The values should vary from 0 to 511 as you turn the pot with a small screwdriver. Try it.

Table 11.1 C Function calls for the A/D converters

Function	Description
`void ad0_enable(void);`	Enable ATD0 for 10 bits
`int adOconv(char ch#);`	Return the average of 4 successive readings of channel *ch#*
`void ad1_enable(void);`	Enable ATD1 for 10 bits
`int ad1conv(char ch#);`	Return the average of 4 successive readings of channel *ch#*

Listing 11.1 Example 11

```
// Example 11: A/D Converter -- Pot
#include <hidef.h>        /* common defines and macros */
#include <mc9s12dg256.h>      /* derivative information */
#pragma LINK_INFO DERIVATIVE "mc9s12dg256b"

#include "main_asm.h" /* interface to the assembly module */

int val;

void main(void) {
  PLL_init();         // set system clock frequency to 24 MHz
  ad0_enable();             // enable a/d converter 0
  lcd_init();               // enable lcd
  while(1) {
    val = ad0conv(7);       // read pot on channel 7
    val = val >> 1;         // shift 1 bit right (divide by 2)
    set_lcd_addr(0x40);     // display on 2nd row of LCD
    write_int_lcd(val);     // write value in field of 5
    ms_delay(100);          // delay 0.1 seconds
  }
}
```

The pinouts of the two A/D converters are shown in Table 11.2.

Table 11.2 Pinouts for A/D Converter

ATD0			ATD1		
Channel No.	Pin Name	Pin No.	Channel No.	Pin Name	Pin No.
0	PADD0	67	0	PAD08	68
1	PADD1	69	1	PAD09	70
2	PADD2	71	2	PAD10	72
3	PADD3	73	3	PAD11	74
4	PADD4	75	4	PAD12	76
5	PADD5	77	5	PAD13	78
6	PADD6	79	6	PAD14	80
7	PADD7	81	7	PAD15	82

PROBLEMS

11.1 Modify Listing 11.1 to display the full 10-bit resolution of the pot reading. What is the range of values displayed?

11.2 Modify Listing 11.1 by dividing the 10-bit reading by 4 before displaying the result on the LCD. What is the range of values displayed?

11.3 Modify Listing 11.1 to display the result in the center of the first row on the LCD.

Example 12

Pulse-Width Modulation (PWM): Motors and Servos

In this example we will show how to control the speed and direction of a DC motor and the position of a servo using the miniDRAGON-Plus2 board.

12.1 Connecting a Motor to a Microcontroller

When connecting a motor or some other load that may draw significant current to a microcontroller it is necessary to use some type of driver circuit. The miniDRAGON-Plus2 board contains a SN754410 quadruple half-H driver. This is a 16-pin chip with the connections shown in Fig. 12.1. Separate power supply connections are provided for the input stage and the output stage of the four tri-state buffers. Jumper J11 will connect the 5 volts of V_{cc} to the input stage. Jumper J12 determines the source of power for the output stage. When using motors it is desirable to use a separate external power supply V_{ext} to provide the current to the motors. Each driver in Fig. 12.1 can output up to 1 ampere of current. You connect the external voltage source to the VEXT lug on the terminal block T4. The SN754410 driver can handle voltages between 4.5 V and 36 V.

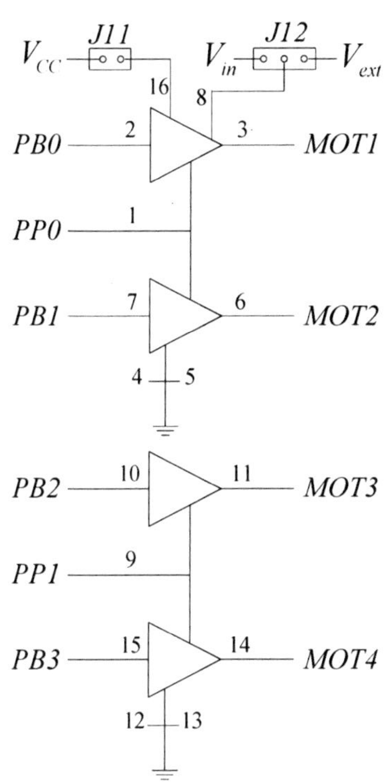

Figure 12.1
SN754410 quadruple half-H driver

The DC motor would be connected between pins *MOT1* and *MOT2* (or between *MOT3* and *MOT4*) in Fig. 12.1. These are labeled on terminal block T4. The two top drivers in Fig. 12.1 are enabled with *PP0*. When *PP0* is 1 the output *MOT1* is high when *PB0* is high and low when *PB0* is low. Similarly, the output *MOT2* is high when *PB0* is high and low when *PB0* is low. When *PP0* is low the outputs *MOT1* and *MOT2* are in the high impedance state. That is, it is the same as disconnecting the motor from the circuit. The lower two drivers in Fig. 12.1 are controlled by PP1 in a similar way.

If a motor is connected between pins *MOT1* and *MOT2* in Fig. 12.1, and if *PB0* is high and *PB1* is low and *PP0* is 1 then the motor will rotate in one direction. If *PB0* is low and *PB1* is high, then current will flow through the motor in the opposite direction and the motor will rotate in the opposite direction. When *PB0* and *PB1* are both high or both low then no current will flow through the motor and the motor will stop.

The speed of a DC motor depends on the voltage applied to the motor – the higher the voltage the faster the motor will turn. If you just wanted to turn on a motor at a constant speed you could connect one side of the motor to *MOT1* in Fig. 12.1 and connect the other side of the motor to ground. In this way you could connect up to four motors to the SN754410 in Fig. 12.1. The polarity of the voltage connected to the motor will determine which way the motor turns. If it is turning the wrong way just exchange the two connections to the motor.

12.2 Controlling the Speed of a DC Motor using PWM

To control the speed of a DC motor using a microcontroller one normally uses a pulse-width modulated signal of the type shown in Fig. 12.2. If this signal is connected to *PP0* in Fig. 12.1 then when the signal is high, current will flow through the motor assuming that *PB0* and *PB1* have different values. When the PWM signal (*PP0*) is low then the motor is disconnected from the circuit and no current flows through the motor.

The period of this pulse train remains constant and the width of the high time, called *duty* in Fig. 12.2, is varied. The *duty cycle* of a PWM signal is defined as the percent time that the signal is high. That is,

$$\text{duty cycle} = \frac{duty}{period} \times 100\%$$

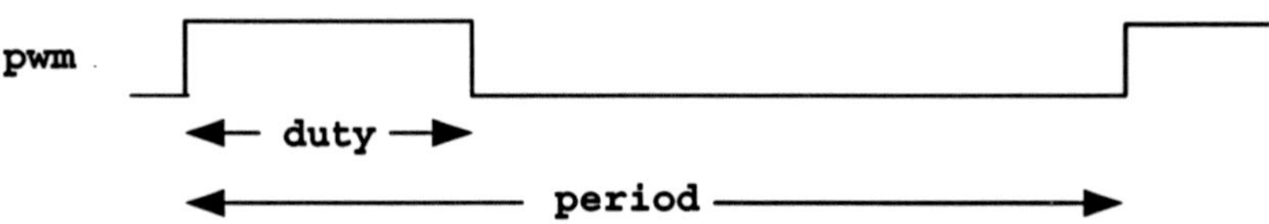

Figure 12.2 A pulse-width modulated signal

The average DC value of the *pwm* signal in Fig. 12.2 will be proportional to the duty cycle. A duty cycle of 100% will have a DC value equal to the maximum value of the *pwm* signal. A duty cycle of 50% will have a DC value equal to half of the maximum value of the *pwm* signal, and so forth. If the voltage across the motor is proportional to this *pwm* signal, then simply changing the pulse width *duty* and therefore the duty cycle changes the speed of the motor.

Port P of the MC9S12DG256 can be used to generate up to eight 8-bit PWM signals or four 16-bit PWM signals. An 8-bit PWM signal will have a resolution of 256 different values of the pulse width *duty*. A 16-bit PWM signal will have a resolution of 65,536 different values of the pulse width *duty*. For speed control of a DC motor an 8-bit PWM signal is usually more than adequate. We provide assembly language routines for generating up to eight different 8-bit PWM signals. For controlling a servo a 16-bit

PWM signal is sometimes needed and we will provide two such routines in the next section.

The SN754410 quadruple half-H driver shown in Fig. 12.1 has internal diodes from the output to V_{ext} and to ground that will eliminate possible voltage spikes that would tend to show up when the current through the motor changes quickly.

The built-in C functions that can be used to control the speed of a DC motor are shown in Table 12.1. A sample program that uses these functions is shown in Listing 12.1. In this example the pot on the miniDRAGON-Plus2 board controls the speed of a DC motor. Pressing pushbutton S1 will set *PB0* to 1 and *PB1* to 0 causing the motor to rotate in one direction (see Fig. 12.1). Pressing pushbutton S2 will set *PB0* to 0 and *PB1* to 1 causing the motor to rotate in the opposite direction. Pressing neither pushbutton or both pushbuttons will stop the motor.

Table 12.1 C function calls for controlling the speed of a DC motor

C Function Call	Meaning
`motor0_init();`	Initialize PWM0 with 10 ms period
`motor1_init();`	Initialize PWM1 with 10 ms period
`motor2_init();`	Initialize PWM2 with 10 ms period
`motor3_init();`	Initialize PWM3 with 10 ms period
`motor4_init();`	Initialize PWM4 with 10 ms period
`motor5_init();`	Initialize PWM5 with 10 ms period
`motor6_init();`	Initialize PWM6 with 10 ms period
`motor7_init();`	Initialize PWM7 with 10 ms period
`motor0(int speed);`	Set speed of motor0 (0 – 255)
`motor1(int speed);`	Set speed of motor1 (0 – 255)
`motor2(int speed);`	Set speed of motor2 (0 – 255)
`motor3(int speed);`	Set speed of motor3 (0 – 255)
`motor4(int speed);`	Set speed of motor4 (0 – 255)
`motor5(int speed);`	Set speed of motor5 (0 – 255)
`motor6(int speed);`	Set speed of motor6 (0 – 255)
`motor7(int speed);`	Set speed of motor7 (0 – 255)

Listing 12.1 Example 12a

```
// Example 12a: Motor speed and direction -- H-Bridge
#include <hidef.h>      /* common defines and macros */
#include <mc9s12dg256.h>      /* derivative information */
#pragma LINK_INFO DERIVATIVE "mc9s12dg256b"

#include "main_asm.h" /* interface to the assembly module */

int val;
int speed;

void main(void) {
  PLL_init();          // set system clock frequency to 24 MHz
  ad0_enable();              // enable a/d converter 0
  lcd_init();                // enable lcd
  SW12_enable();             // enable switches S1 and S2
  motor0_init();             // enable 8-bit pwm0 for motor
  while(1) {
    if(SW1_down())           // motor on clockwise
       PORTB |= 0x01;        // PB0 = 1
    else
       PORTB &= 0xFE;        // PB0 = 0
    if(SW2_down())           // motor on counter-clockwise
       PORTB |= 0x02;        // PB1 = 1
    else
       PORTB &= 0xFD;        // PB1 = 0
    val = ad0conv(7);       // read pot on channel 7; 0 - 1023
    speed = val >> 2;       // shift 2 bit right; 0 - 255
    motor0(speed);           // set motor speed
    set_lcd_addr(0x40);     // display on 2nd row of LCD
    write_int_lcd(speed);          // write value in field of 5
    ms_delay(100);                 // delay 0.1 seconds
  }
}
```

12.3 Controlling the Position of a Servo using PWM

A servo motor is a special type of device that contains a DC motor, some gears, a potentiometer, and electronic circuitry for position feedback control, all packaged in a single compact device. These servos are widely used in model airplanes and radio controlled cars and are therefore mass produced and very inexpensive. A typical servo of this type, the Futaba S3004, is shown in Fig. 12.3. This servo has three wires attached to it: the red wire goes to +5 volts, the black wire goes to ground, and the white wire goes to a PWM signal that controls the position of the motor shaft.

Figure 12.3
The Futaba S3004 servo

The motor shaft is prevented from moving more than about 90 degrees by limit stops. The PWM signal used to control the position of a servo is shown in Fig. 12.4. Note that the period if fixed at 20 ms and the pulse width varies from about 1.1 ms to 1.9 ms in order to move the shaft position through a total angle of about 90 degrees.

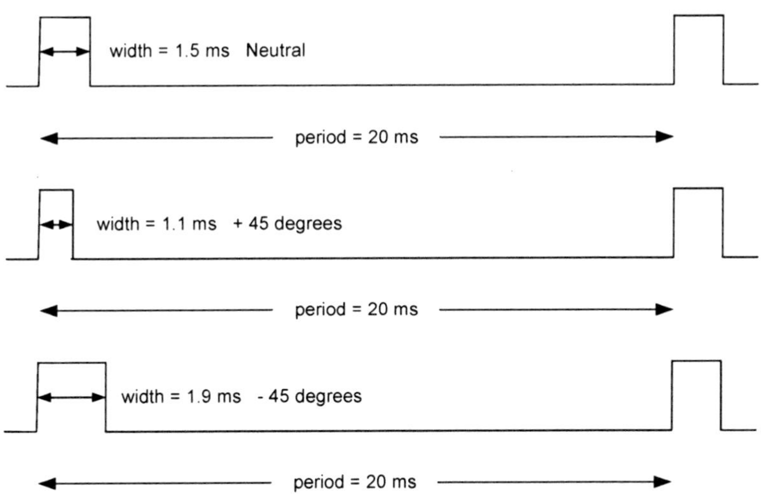

Figure 12.4 PWM signals for controlling the position of a servo

Inasmuch as the useful duty cycle of this PWM signal varies from only about 5 to 10 percent we will use the 16-bit option with a 3 MHz PWM clock in order to provide a resolution of 60,000 over the 20 ms period. In this case the value of *duty* in Fig. 12.2 would be about 4560 for the neutral position, 3360 for the +45 degree position, and 5760 for the –45 degree position.

The built-in C functions that can be used to control the position of a servo are shown in Table 12.2. A sample program that uses these functions is shown in Listing 12.2. In this example the pot on the miniDRAGON-Plus2 board controls the position of a servo and displays the *width* value on the LCD.

Table 12.2 C function calls for controlling the position of a servo

C Function Call	Meaning
`servo54_init();`	Initialize PWM5 with 20 ms period
`servo76_init();`	Initialize PWM7 with 20 ms period
`set_servo54(int width);`	Set position of servo5 (3300 – 5700)
`set_servo76(int width);`	Set position of servo7 (3300 – 5700)

To use the program in Listing 12.2 connect the servo connector to header J9 with the white wire next to header J7. Connect an external 5 volt power supply to the EXT lugs next to the pot. The position of the servo and the value on the LCD will change as you turn the pot.

Listing 12.2 Example 12b

```
// Example 12b: Servo demo with pot
#include <hidef.h>      /* common defines and macros */
#include <mc9s12dg256.h>     /* derivative information */
#pragma LINK_INFO DERIVATIVE "mc9s12dg256b"

#include "main_asm.h" /* interface to the assembly module */

void main(void) {
  int val;
  int width;

  PLL_init();       // set system clock frequency to 24 MHz
  ad0_enable();                // enable a/d converter 0
  lcd_init();                  // enable lcd
  servo76_init();              // enable pwm1 for servo
  while(1) {
    val = ad0conv(7);          // 0 - 1023
    width = (val << 1) + 3477; // width: 3477 - 5523
    set_lcd_addr(0x40);        // line 2 of lcd display
    write_int_lcd(width);      // display width on lcd
    set_servo76(width);        // move servo to pos width
  }
}
```

A second sample program that continually rotates the servo back and forth through an angle of about 90 degrees is shown in Listing 12.3. You can experiment with this program by changing the *for* loop values and the delay time.

Listing 12.3 Example 12c

```
// Example 12c: Servo demo with for loop
#include <hidef.h>      /* common defines and macros */
#include <mc9s12dg256.h>     /* derivative information */
#pragma LINK_INFO DERIVATIVE "mc9s12dg256b"

#include "main_asm.h" /* interface to the assembly module */

void main(void) {
  int width;
  PLL_init();       // set system clock frequency to 24 MHz
  servo76_init();              // enable pwm1 for servo
  while(1) {
    for(width = 4500; width <= 6000; width = width + 5){
      set_servo76(width);      // move servo from 4500 to 6000
      ms_delay(5);
    }
    for(width = 6000; width >= 3000; width = width - 5){
      set_servo76(width);      // move servo from 6000 to 3000
      ms_delay(5);
    }
    for(width = 3000; width < 4500; width = width + 5){
      set_servo76(width);      // move servo from 3000 to 4500
      ms_delay(5);
    }
  }
}
```

Example 13

The Serial Peripheral Interface (SPI)

In this example we will show how the serial peripheral interface (SPI) can be used to read up to 16 switches or a hex keypad.

13.1 Operation of the SPI

Two different methods of serial communications are available on HCS12 microcontrollers. We have already seen the use of the serial communications interface (SCI) in Example 8, which uses start and stop bits to synchronize each transmitted character. The second method of serial communications is the serial peripheral interface (SPI), which is a synchronous serial interface in which a clock signal is sent along with the data signal.

The SPI is a synchronous serial interface in which data in an 8-bit byte can be shifted in and/or out one bit at a time. It can be used to communicate with a serial peripheral device or with another microcontroller with an SPI interface. The MC9S12DG256 has three SPI modules that behave the same. Each module contains four signals as shown in Table 13.1. The pin numbers in parentheses in Table 13.1 are the MC9S12DG256 pin numbers. The system can operate in either a master or slave mode. When communicating with a peripheral device the MC9S12DG256 SPI will operate as the master. When one MC9S12DG256 (the master) is connected to a second MC9S12DG256 (the slave) the four SPI signals will be connected as shown in Fig. 13.1.

Table 13.1 MC9S12DP256 SPI Signals

Pin	SPI signal	Name
SPI0		
PS4 (93)	MISO0	Master-In-Slave-Out
PS5 (94)	MOSI0	Master-Out-Slave-In
PS6 (95)	SCK0	Serial Clock
PS7 (96)	SS0	Slave Select
SPI1		
PP0 (4)	MISO1	Master-In-Slave-Out
PP1 (3)	MOSI1	Master-Out-Slave-In
PP2 (2)	SCK1	Serial Clock
PP3 (1)	SS1	Slave Select
SPI2		
PP4 (112)	MISO2	Master-In-Slave-Out
PP5 (111)	MOSI2	Master-Out-Slave-In
PP7 (109)	SCK2	Serial Clock
PP6 (110)	SS2	Slave Select

In the master the bits are sent out the *MOSI* (master out - slave in) pin and received in the *MISO* (master in - slave out) pin. In the slave the bits are received in the *MOSI* (master out - slave in) pin and sent out the *MISO* (master in - slave out) pin. The bits to be shifted out are stored in the SPI data register, *SP0DR*, and by default are sent out most-significant bit (bit 7) first as shown in Figure 13.1. By programming a bit in one of the control registers the bits can be sent out least significant bit first. At the same time that bit 7 is being shifted out the *MOSI* pin in the master a bit from bit 7 of the slave is being shifted into bit 0 of the master via the *MISO* pin. This bit will eventually end up in bit 7 of the master after eight clock pulses or shifts. The clock which controls how fast the bits are shifted out of and into *SP0DR* is the signal *SCK*. The frequency of this clock can be controlled by the SPI baud rate register. The *SS* (slave-select) pin must be low to select a slave. This signal can come from any pin on the master, including its *SS* pin when it is configured as an output.

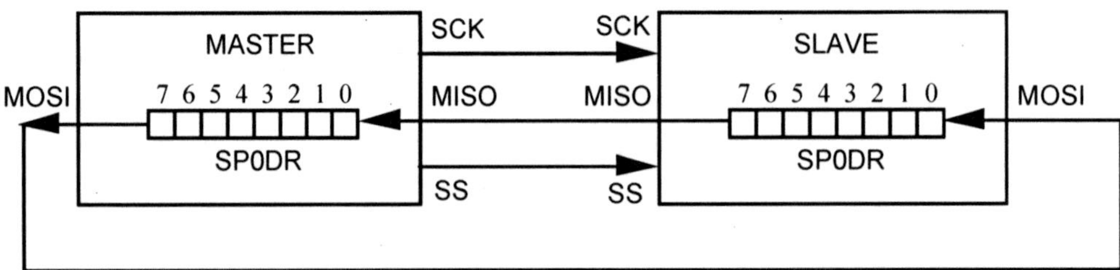

Figure 13.1 Two SPI modules connected in a master-slave configuration

13.2 Programming the SPI in C

To make it easy to use the SPI ports we have written assembly language routines that can be called using the C functions shown in Table 13.2. There are four functions associated with each of the three SPI modules ($x = 0, 1, 2$). The function *SPIx_init()* will initialize the SPI port as a master and set the clock rate to 250 kHz.

The function *send_SPIx(c)* will send a byte out the *MOSI* pin, wait for the transfer to be complete, and then return the value of the byte shifted into the data register. Finally, the functions *SSx_HI()* and *SSx_LO()* set the corresponding *SS* pin high and low.

To send a byte of data out the *SPI0 MOSI* pin you just need to put the byte in a character *c* and call the function *send_SPI0(c)*. Note that when you do this a new byte will come into the SPI data register, *SP0DR*, from the *MISO* pin. This may or may not be meaningful data depending on whether that pin is connected to some peripheral. Similarly, the byte you send out the *MOSI* pin may or may not be meaningful depending on whether that pin is connected to some peripheral. In the next section we will illustrate the use of the SPI port to read data from shift registers.

For convenience, the signals associated with SPI0 are brought out to header J4 next to the pushbutton switches S1 and S2. Check the miniDRAGON-Plus2 schematics for specific pin locations.

Table 13.2 C Function calls for the SPI ports

Function	Description
`void SPI0_init(void);`	Initialize SPI0 with baud rate of 250 kHz
`char send_SPI0(char c);`	Send character *c* out SCI0; returns character shifted in
`void SS0_HI(void);`	Set SS0 (PS7, pin 95) HI
`void SS0_LO(void);`	Set SS0 (PS7, pin 95) LO
`void SPI1_init();`	Initialize SPI1 with baud rate of 250 kHz
`char send_SPI1(char c);`	Send character *c* out SCI1; returns character shifted in
`void SS1_HI(void);`	Set SS1 (PP3, pin 1) HI
`void SS1_LO(void);`	Set SS1 (PP3, pin 1) LO
`void SPI2_init();`	Initialize SPI2 with baud rate of 250 kHz
`char send_SPI2(char c);`	Send character *c* out SCI2; returns character shifted in
`void SS2_HI(void);`	Set SS2 (PP6, pin 110) HI
`void SS2_LO(void);`	Set SS2 (PP6, pin 110) LO

13.3 Keypad Interfacing with 74165 Shift Registers

Keypad interfacing was described in Example 6. In that example the keypad was in the form of a 4 x 4 matrix. Some keypads have an alternate form in which one side of each key is connected to a common ground. In this example we will show how the SPI port can be used to read this type of 16 x 1 hex keypad by using 74165 shift registers.

A 16 x 1 hex keypad (or any collection of 16 switches) can be connected to two 74165 shift registers as shown in Figure 13.2. In this case one side of each switch is connected to ground. The 74165 is an 8-bit parallel in/serial out shift register. The other side of each switch is connected to one of the parallel inputs (*A–H*) of the shift register. If pin 1 (*SH/!LD*) of the 74165 is brought low the values on the eight parallel inputs are latched into the shift register. When the *SH/!LD* pin is high and the *CLK INH* pin is low then on the rising edge of the *CLK* input the eight bits in the shift register are shifted one bit to the right. Bit *A* is shifted to *B*, *B* to *C*, etc. Bit *G* is shifted to *H* which shows up on the serial output pin, Q_H. In Figure 13.2 the output Q_H of the lower 74165 is connected to the serial input pin, *SER*, of the upper 74165. The output Q_H of the upper 74165 is connected to the *MISO* pin of one of the SPI ports in the MC9S12DG256.

In Figure 13.2 the SPI signal *SCK* is connected to each *CLK* pin of the two 74165 chips and the SPI signal *SS* is connected to each *SH/!LD* pin of the two 74165 chips. Note that the *MOSI* pin of the SPI port is not connected to anything. We are only interested in receiving bytes in the *MISO* pin. To do this, of course, we must write a dummy value (say zero) to the SPI data register, *SP0DR*, (by calling our C function *send_SPI0(0)*) and it will be shifted out the unconnected *MOSI* pin at the same time that the desired byte is being shifted in the *MISO* pin.

Notice in Figure 13.2 that pin *H* of the upper 74165 (key 3) will be the first bit shifted out. This will end up in the most-significant bit of the first byte transferred. After transferring one byte the register contents of the lower 74165 will have been shifted into the upper 74165 shift register. The value associated with key 7 will now be at the output Q_H of the upper 74165. After a second byte is transferred this key 7 value will be at the most-significant bit location of this second byte. If the first byte transferred becomes the most-significant byte of a 16-bit word then the bits of this 16-bit integer will be associated with the 16 hex key values as indicated in Figure 13.3.

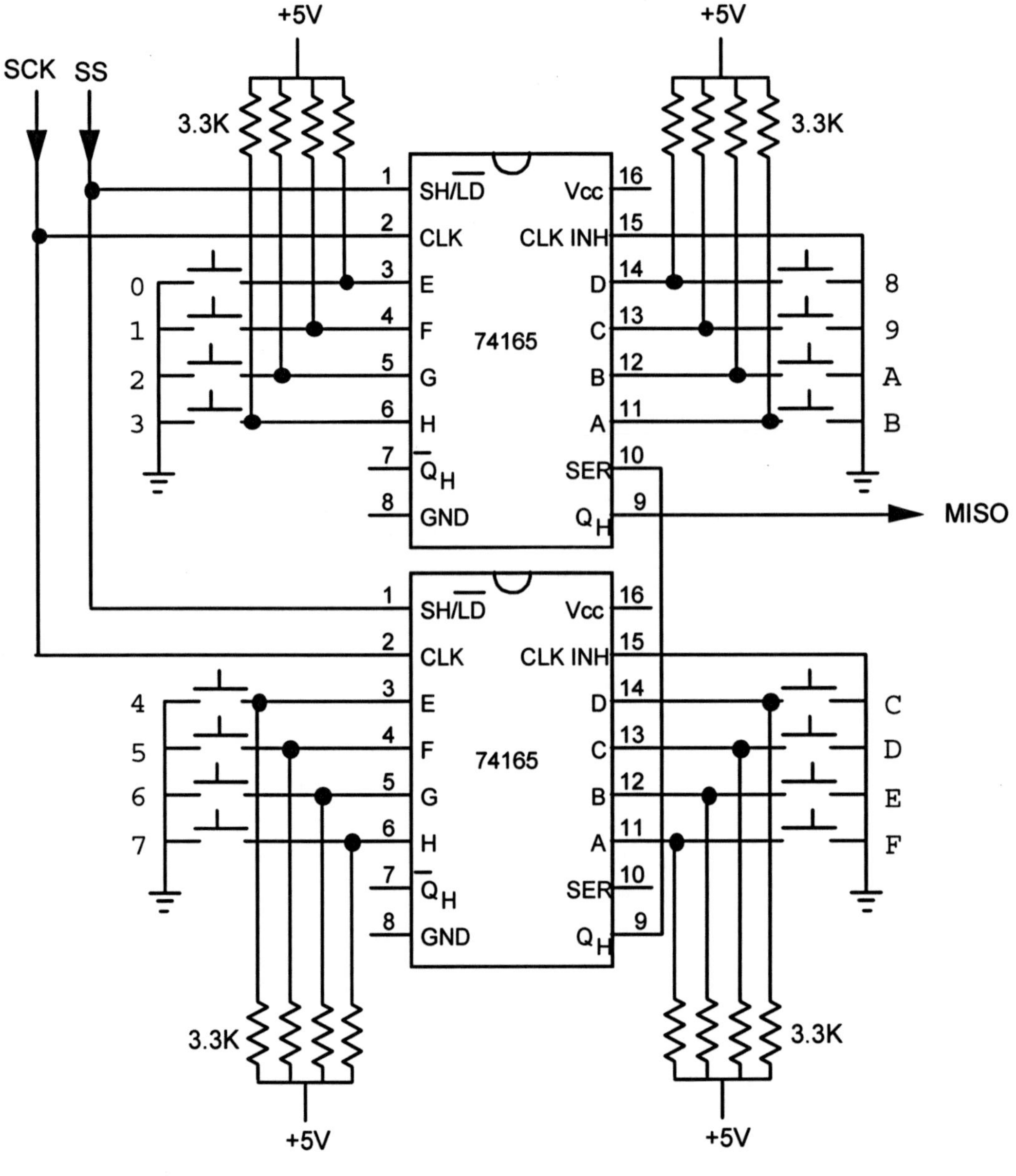

Figure 13.2 Connecting a 16 x 1 hex keypad to two 74165 shift registers

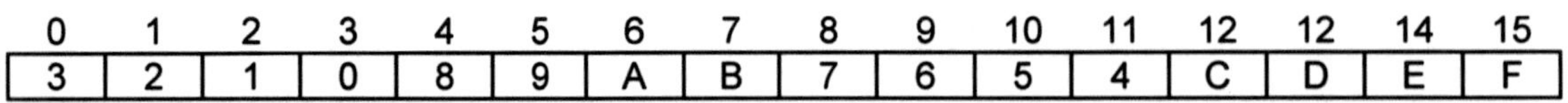

0	1	2	3	4	5	6	7	8	9	10	11	12	12	14	15
3	2	1	0	8	9	A	B	7	6	5	4	C	D	E	F

Figure 13.3 Keypad hex values after transferring 16 bits in Figure 13.2

The C function *read_16shift()* shown in Listing 13.1 will return the 16-bit value shown in Figure 13.3. It does this by shifting in two 8-bit bytes through the SPI port. Note that the high byte is read first, shifted 8 bits to the left, and then ORed with the low byte.

Listing 13.1 read_16shift() function

```
int read_16shift(void){
  int    data;
  char   c;
     SS0_LO();                // latch data
     SS0_HI();
     c = send_SPI0(0);       // get 1st byte by sending dummy data
     data = c;
     data = data << 8;
     c = send_SPI0(0);       // get 2nd byte by sending dummy data
     data = data | c;
     return data;
}
```

Note from Figure 13.2 that if no key is being pressed then all of the parallel inputs to the shift registers are pulled high. This means that all of the bits in Figure 13.3 will be set to 1. Thus, the value of this 16-bit value will be $FFFF. If any key was being pressed when the function *read_16shift()* is executed then the bit associated with that key will be zero. The function *get_key( )* shown in Listing 13.2 will search for the bit in Figure 13.3 that is cleared to zero. It does this by ANDing *data* with a mask with only a single bit set and checking to see if that bit was zero. The mask starts with the most-significant bit set (0x8000) which corresponds to bit number 0 in Figure 13.3 and then shifts the bit right each time through the *while* loop by using the statement

```
mask >>= 1;
```

which is equivalent to

```
mask = mask >> 1;
```

We label the most-significant bit in Figure 13.3 as 0 rather that 15 so that this bit number will correspond to the index value in the table *keytbl[]* shown in Listing 13.2. When a zero bit value is found, the value of *keytbl[i]* will be the hex value of the key being pressed and this value is returned as the value of the function *get_key()*. Note that if no key is being pressed the value of *get_key()* is 16.

Listing 13.3 shows a main program that will use the two functions given in Listings 13.1 and 13.2. This program will wait for you to press a key and then display the key value of the LCD.

Listing 13.2 get_key() function

```
char get_key(){
  const char keytbl[] = {
    0x3, 0x2, 0x1, 0x0,
    0x8, 0x9, 0xA, 0xB,
    0x7, 0x6, 0x5, 0x4,
    0xC, 0xD, 0xE, 0xF
  };
  int mask;
  int data;
  int i;
  char found;
  char key;
      data = read_16shift();
      mask = 0x8000;
      found = 0;
      i = 0;
      key = 16;           // not found if key = 16
      while((i < 16) && (found == 0)){
        if((data & mask) == 0){
          found = 1;
          key = keytbl[i];
        }
        else {
          mask >>= 1;
          i++;
        }
      }
      return key;
}
```

Listing 13.3 Example 13

```
// Example 13: SPI Keypad Interfacing with 74165 Shift Registers
#include <hidef.h>      /* common defines and macros */
#include <mc9s12dp256.h>     /* derivative information */
#include "main_asm.h" /* interface to the assembly module */
#pragma LINK_INFO DERIVATIVE "mc9s12dp256b"
int read_16shift(void);
char get_key(void);

void main(void) {
  char key;
  PLL_init();          // set system clock frequency to 24 MHz
  lcd_init();             // enable lcd
  SPI0_init();            // enable SPI0
  set_lcd_addr(0x40);
  while(1) {
    key = get_key();
    if(key < 16){
      key = hex2asc(key); // convert to ascii
      data8(key);         // display on lcd
    }
  }
}
```

PROBLEMS

13.1 The Analog Devices AD7376 is a ±15 V Operation Digital Potentiometer. A simplified block diagram is shown below.

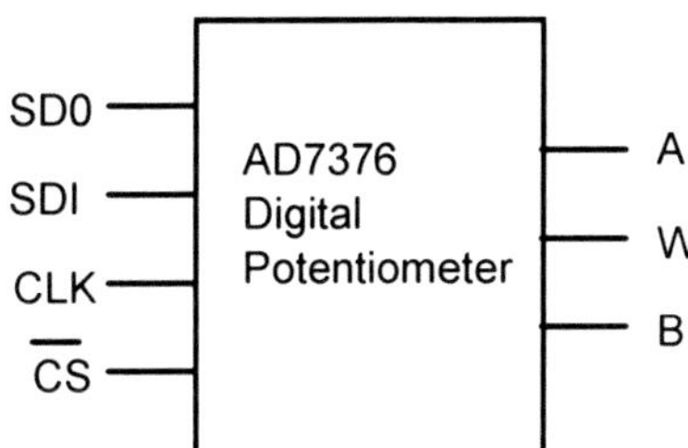

You can go to http://www.analog.com/en/prod/0,,761_797_AD7376%2C00.html to download the full data sheet. The fixed resistance between *A* and *B*, R_{AB}, can be either 10 kΩ, 50 kΩ, 100 kΩ, or 1 MΩ. The output *W* is the "wiper" that causes the resistance between W and B to be given by the equation

$$R_{WB}(D) = (D/128)xR_{AB} + R_W$$

where *D* is 7-bit data that has been shifted into *SDI* and R_W is the wiper contact resistance equal to 120 Ω.

You can interface the AD7376 to an SPI port by connecting the SPI *SS* signal to the *CS* pin, the *SCK* signal to the *CLK* pin, the *MOSI* signal to the *SDI* pin, and the *MISO* signal to the *SD0* pin. When *CS* is low 8-bit data is shifted into *SDI*, MSB first. Each bit is latched on the rising edge of the clock that idles low. The *SD0* pin can be connected to the *SDI* pin of a second AD7376 to daisy-chain multiple variable resistors.

Write a C function called *R(int n)* that will cause the resistance between *W* and *B* to be *n* ohms. Assume that R_{AB} = 10 kΩ, so that *n* should be between 0 and 10,000.

Example 14

Real-time Interrupts

In this example we will introduce the idea of interrupts and show how to use the real-time interrupt to create a count variable that increments every 10 milliseconds.

14.1 Hardware Interrupts

Hardware interrupts allow external events to interrupt the normal execution of a program and instead execute an interrupt service routine, after which the execution of the original program is picked up where it left off. The addresses of the interrupt service routines are called *interrupt vectors*. These interrupt vectors are stored in a special table in memory. When a particular interrupt occurs the address of the interrupt service routine is looked up in the interrupt vector table and control is transferred to that address.

There are over 50 different sources of interrupts on a MC9S12DG256 and their interrupt vectors are stored in memory between the hex addresses $FF80 and $FFFF. (We will sometimes use a $ sign instead of 0x to indicate a hexadecimal value.) The most important interrupt vector is the reset vector that is located at addresses $FFFE and $FFFF. When the *RESET* pin on an HCS12 microcontroller goes low, normal microprocessor functions are suspended. When this pin returns high the microprocessor will disable hardware interrupts and start executing instructions starting at the address stored at $FFFE-$FFFF. HCS12 microcontrollers have a power-on reset (POR) circuit that causes the reset signal to be asserted internally after power (5 volts) has been applied to the processor.

It is necessary for addresses $FFFE-$FFFF to be in some type of non-volatile memory (ROM, EPROM, or Flash memory) so that a valid reset vector will be at that address. Of course, the memory it points to must also be in non-volatile memory so that some meaningful code will be executed when you turn on the processor. In the DRAGON12-Plus the memory between $F800 and $FFFF is in protected flash memory and contains the Serial Monitor in addition to the table of interrupt vectors.[1] The reset vector at $FFFE - $FFFF contains the address $F800 which is the beginning of the Serial Monitor. If the left slide switch SW7 is set to LOAD then when you press the reset button the Serial Monitor at $F800 will be executed. When you download your program to the flash memory using CodeWarrior the Serial Monitor maps the interrupt vector table between $FF80 - $FFFF to unprotected flash memory between $F780 - $F7FF and stores the starting address of your program at $F7FE - $F7FF. If the left slide switch SW7 is set to RUN then when you press the reset button your program whose address is at $F7FE - $F7FF will be executed.

---

[1] You must order the miniDRAGON-Plus2 with Serial Monitor included; otherwise, by default, it comes with a Debug12 monitor installed.

A hardware interrupt is an unexpected event that can occur at any time during the execution of a program. It might result from pressing a key, having a byte received in the SCI port, or when some timer has timed out. When a hardware interrupt occurs a series of events takes place. The current instruction is completed and then the programming registers (see Fig. B.1 in Appendix B) are pushed on the stack. The return address will be the value in the program counter; i.e., the address of the instruction following the one being executed when the interrupt occurs. This will be the address returned to after the interrupt service routine is executed. After all registers in Fig. B.1 are pushed on the stack, both the *I* bit and the *X* bit in the condition code register *CCR* are set This means that another interrupt cannot get serviced during the execution of the interrupt service routine. The address of the interrupt service routine is loaded from the interrupt vector table into the program counter so that the first instruction in the interrupt service routine will be executed. The last instruction of an interrupt service routine is the *RTI* instruction, which will pop the registers shown in Fig. B.1 off the stack, including the *CCR* register which will have its *I* bit cleared. At that point a new interrupt can occur including one that might have occurred during the processing of the previous interrupt.

A list of all interrupt sources available on the MC9S12DG256 is given in Table D.1 in Appendix D. Note that each interrupt source has a vector number (between 0 and 57) associated with it. The address of the interrupt vector for each interrupt source is also shown in Table D.1.

To use an interrupt it is first necessary to write an interrupt service routine that will be executed when the interrupt occurs. To write a real-time interrupt routine in C and tell it where the interrupt vector is stored you would use the following form

```
void interrupt 7 handler(){
  << your C code goes here >>
}
```

The word *interrupt* tells the C compiler that this is an interrupt service routine and the number 7 is the interrupt vector number from Table D.1. In this case the 7 is the vector number for a *real-time interrupt* with the interrupt vector stored in addresses $FFF0 - $FFF1. The name of the interrupt service routine is *handler()*. The compiler will automatically assign the address of this interrupt routine to the proper interrupt vector address. When using the Serial Monitor and CodeWarrior these interrupt vector addresses have been mapped to $F780 - $F7FF. Thus, you will find the address of the real-time interrupt service routine *handler()* at addresses $F7F0 - $F7F1.

14.2 Real-Time Interrupts

As an example of using interrupts we will write a program that uses the *real-time interrupt*, which produces an interrupt at periodic intervals. We have written three assembly language routines for real-time interrupts that can be called using the C fuctions shown in Table 14.1. The routine *RTI_init()* enables a real-time interrupt that produces an interrupt every 10.24 milliseconds. When an interrupt occurs it sets a flag in one of the RTI registers. You must clear this flag in the interrupt service routine so as not to cause another interrupt immediately upon leaving the interrupt service routine. The C function *clear_RTI_flag()* will do this. An example of using the real-time interrupt in a C program is shown in Listing 14.1. The C function *RTI_disable()* will disable real-time interrupts.

In this program two global variables, *ticks* and *ticks0*, are defined as unsigned short (16-bit) integers. The interrupt service routine is

```
// RTI Interrupt Service Routine
void interrupt 7 handler(){
  ticks++;
  clear_RTI_flag();
}
```

which just increments the variable *ticks* every 10.24 ms and the clears the RTI flag.

Table 14.1 C Function calls for the real-time interrupt

Function	Description
`void RTI_init(void);`	Initialize real-time interrupts every 10.24 ms
`void clear_RTI_flag(void)`	Clear the RTI flag
`void RTI_disable(void)`	Disable real-time interrupts

Listing 14.1 Example 14

```
// Example 14: Real-time interrupt
#include <hidef.h>      /* common defines and macros */
#include <mc9s12dg256.h>     /* derivative information */
#pragma LINK_INFO DERIVATIVE "mc9s12dg256b"

#include "main_asm.h" /* interface to the assembly module */

void half_sec_delay(void);

unsigned short ticks, ticks0; // RTI interrupt counts

// RTI Interrupt Service Routine
void interrupt 7 handler(){
  ticks++;
  clear_RTI_flag();
}

void main(void) {
  PLL_init();             // set system clock frequency to 24 MHz
  seg7_enable();          // enable 7-segment displays
  RTI_init();
  while(1) {
    seg7dec(8);           //    display 8 on 7seg display #3
    half_sec_delay();
    seg7_off();           //    turn off 7seg display
    half_sec_delay();
  }
}

void half_sec_delay(void){    // delay for 0.5 seconds
  ticks0 = ticks;
  while((ticks-ticks0)<49) {
  }
}
```

Note in Listing 14.1 we have defined the function *half_second_delay()* that first reads the current value of *ticks* (that is being incremented every 10.24 ms by the real-time interrupt routine) and stores this value in *ticks0*. It then stays in the *while* loop as long as (*ticks* – *ticks0*) is less than 49. Thus, the *while* loop will exit after 49 interrupts which will take 49 x 10.24 ms = 0.502 seconds. Remember that *ticks* is being incremented in the background by the real-time interrupt routine. Once you enable this real-time interrupt by calling *RTI_init()* the value of *ticks* gets incremented every 10.24 ms.

The main program in Listing 14.1 just blinks the digit 8 on the 7-segment display on and off every second.

PROBLEMS

14.1 Modify Listing 14.1 to have the digit 2 blink once every 2 seconds. That is, it should be on for one second and off for one second.

14.2 Write a program that will blink the Morse code SOS on the rightmost 7-segment display. The program should first blink an S for three short blinks (dot-dot-dot), then blink an O for three long blinks (dash-dash-dash), and then blink the S again for three short blinks (dot-dot-dot). Repeat this sequence endlessly after a short pause.

Example 15

Interrupt-Driven Controller

In this example we will use the real-time interrupt of Example 14 to produce arbitrary delays in an arbitrary number of states.

15.1 Interrupt-Driven Traffic Light

It is often useful to be able to sequence through an arbitrary number of states, staying in each state an arbitrary amount of time. For example, consider the set of traffic lights shown in Figure 15.1. The lights are assumed to be at a four-way intersection with one street going north-south and the other road going east-west.

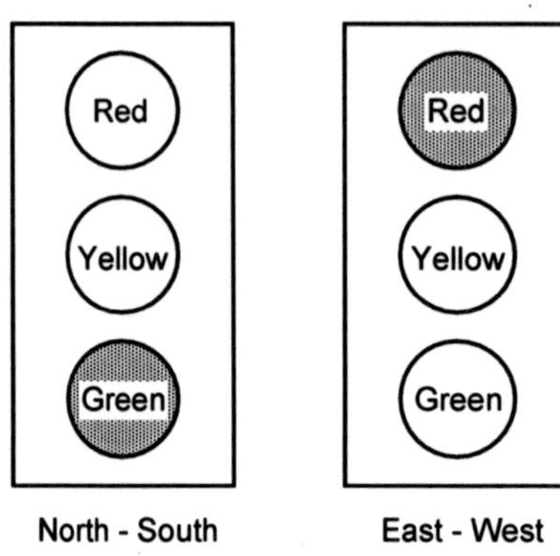

Figure 15.1 Six colored LEDs can represent a set of traffic lights

To simulate these traffic lights we could use colored LEDs and connect them to Port M as shown in Figure 15.2. When the pin output is low the output of the inverter is high (+5 volts) and no current can flow through the LED and therefore no light will be emitted. If we bring the port output pin high, the output of the inverter goes low (assume about 0.2 volts) and current will flow from the +5 volt power supply through the resistor *R* and the LED. The resistor is used to limit the amount of current that flows through the LED. A typical current would be 15 milliamps or 15 x 10^{-3} amps. Using Ohm's law we can compute the resistor size needed as shown in Figure 15.1. You could, for example, connect the east-west lights to *PM0–PM2* and the north-south lights to *PM3–PM5*.

We can use real-time interrupts (see Example 14) to continually cycle through the six states shown in Table 15.1. Note that when the light on one street is red and the light on the other street is green we will delay 5 seconds. (Assume very fast cars so that you won't have to wait all day!) We will delay 1 second on a yellow-red or red-red combination.

The idea is to use interrupts so that the entire operation will be carried out in the background with no need for the CPU to intervene to keep the traffic lights going. The same idea can be used to cycle through any set of states that you can change by writing to an output port.

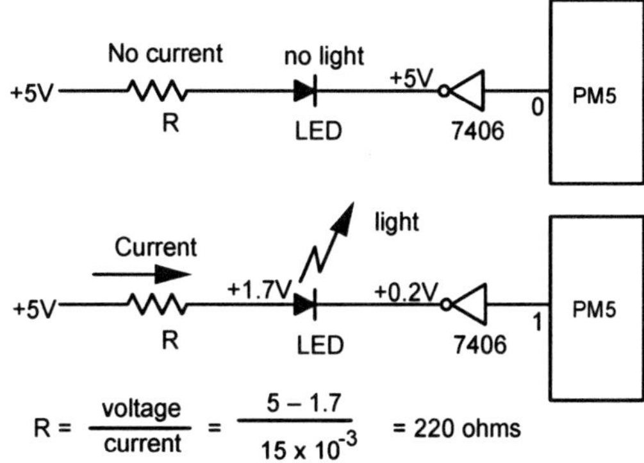

Figure 15.2 Turning on an LED by storing a 1 in PM5

Table 15.1 Traffic Light States

State	North - South	East - West	Delay (sec.)
0	Green	Red	5
1	Yellow	Red	1
2	Red	Red	1
3	Red	Green	5
4	Red	Yellow	1
5	Red	Red	1

We begin by defining two arrays that represents the six states shown in Table 15.1. These arrays are called *PortH[]* and *delay[]* in the program shown in Listing 15.1. (We'll use Port H in Listing 15.1 so you can see the results on the segments of the 7-segment display.) The first byte in the array *PortH[]* is the hex value 0xF3. This is the binary value 11110011 which will be written out to Port H. The bits in Port M will be assigned to the colored LEDs according to the bit positions --RYGRYG. Thus the hex value 0x0C will turn on the green north-south light and the red east-west light.

The first entry in the array *delay[]* is the delay time measured in *ticks*. A tick will be the time between interrupts, which is 10.24 ms. Therefore, a delay of 1 second will be 488 ticks and a delay of 5 seconds will be 98 ticks. The rest of the entries is the *PortH[]* array store the values to be written to Port M for each state and the corresponding entries in the *delay[]* array contain the delay time for that state.

The variable *dtime* defined at the beginning of the program in Listing 15.1 is used to hold the number of *ticks* before a timeout that will move to the next state. This value will be initialized to 1 so that a state change will occur on the first interrupt. The variable *ix* will be the index into the states.

The interrupt service routine, *handler()*, shown in Listing 15.1 starts by decrementing the value of *dtime*. If the decremented value is not zero then the *IF* statement is skipped and the *RTIF* flag is cleared.

If the decremented value of *dtime* is equal to zero in the interrupt service routine, then the *IF* statement is executed. The first statement turns on the next set of lights by writing the value of *PortH[ix]* to *PTH.* The next statement stores the corresponding delay time for that state in *dtime*. The state index *ix* is then incremented and when it equals the number of states (6) it is reset to zero.

Listing 15.1 Example 15a

```
//  Example 15a  Traffic Lights
#include <hidef.h>      /* common defines and macros */
#include <mc9s12dg256.h>     /* derivative information */
#pragma LINK_INFO DERIVATIVE "mc9s12dg256b"

#include "main_asm.h" /* interface to the assembly module */

int dtime;                  // delay time
int ix;                     // index into states
const int numstates = 6;
const char PortH[] = {      // --RYGRYG
      0xF3,                 // 11110011
      0xEB,                 // 11101011
      0xDB,                 // 11011011
      0xDE,                 // 11011110
      0xDD,                 // 11011101
      0xDB,                 // 11011011
};
const int delay[] = {
      488,                    // 5 sec delay
      98,                     // 1 sec delay
      98,                     // 1 sec delay
      488,                    // 5 sec delay
      98,                     // 1 sec delay
      98,                     // 1 sec delay
};

void interrupt 7 handler(){
  dtime--;
  if(dtime == 0){
    PTH = PortH[ix];        // turn on next lights
    dtime = delay[ix];      // get next delay time
    ix++;                   // increment index
    if(ix == numstates){    // after going through all states
      ix = 0;               //  reset index to 0
    }
  }
  clear_RTI_flag();
}

void main(void) {
  PLL_init();         // set system clock frequency to 24 MHz
  DDRH = 0xFF;        // all bits of Port H are outputs
  RTI_init();         // initialize RTI to 10.24 ms interrupts
  ix = 0;             // reset index into states
  dtime = 1;          // start traffic light right away
  while(1) {          // do nothing while traffic light goes
  }
}
```

In the main program the data direction register of Port H is set for all outputs, the real-time interrupts are enabled, *ix* is set to 0 and *dtime* is set to 1. The main program then just enters an infinite *while* loop. The interrupt routine takes care of changing the traffic lights on schedule. The main program could go on and do useful things while the traffic light is changing all on its own!

15.2 Interrupt-Driven Blinking SOS

As a second example of an interrupt-driven controller that you can run on the miniDRAGON-Plus2 board without adding external components, let's write a program to blink the Morse Code for SOS on the 7-segment display while displaying the letters SOS (see Problem 14.2). The Morse Code for S is *dot-dot-dot* and that for O is *dash-dash-dash.* We will therefore blink an S three times quickly to indicate *dot-dot-dot* and then blink an O about 3 times slower to indicate *dash-dash-dash* and then blink an S again three times quickly to indicate another *dot-dot-dot*. This sequence will then be repeated endlessly.

A program for doing this is shown in Listing 15.2. Note that it follows the same pattern that we used for the traffic light example in Listing 15.1. In this case there are a total of 18 states: 6 to turn the S on and off three times; 6 to turn the O on and off three times; and 6 to turn the S on and off three times again. The on and off delay time for the dot is 12 x 10.24 ms = 0.123 seconds and the on and off delay time for the dash is 36 x 10.24 ms = 0.369 seconds. A slightly longer delay is used at the end of the first three dots and an even longer delay is used at the end of the entire SOS sequence. Try this program.

Listing 15.2 Example 15b

```
// Example 15b: Interrupt-Driven Controller: SOS
#include <hidef.h>      /* common defines and macros */
#include <mc9s12dg256.h>     /* derivative information */
#pragma LINK_INFO DERIVATIVE "mc9s12dg256b"

#include "main_asm.h" /* interface to the assembly module */

unsigned short dtime;     // delay time
int ix;                   // index into states
const int numstates = 18;
const char seg7[] = {
  0x12, 0x7F, 0x12, 0x7F, 0x12, 0x7F,   // S
  0x40, 0x7F, 0x40, 0x7F, 0x40, 0x7F,   // O
  0x12, 0x7F, 0x12, 0x7F, 0x12, 0x7F,   // S
};
const char delay[] = {
  0x0C, 0x0C, 0x0C, 0x0C, 0x0C, 0x18,   // dots
  0x24, 0x24, 0x24, 0x24, 0x24, 0x24,   // dashes
  0x0C, 0x0C, 0x0C, 0x0C, 0x0C, 0x30,   // dots
};

void interrupt 7 handler(){
  dtime--;
  if(dtime == 0){
    seg7_on(seg7[ix]);      // turn on next display
    dtime = delay[ix];      // get next delay time
    ix++;                   // increment index
    if(ix == numstates){    // after going through all states
      ix = 0;               //  reset index to 0
    }
  }
  clear_RTI_flag();
}

void main(void) {
  PLL_init();        // set system clock frequency to 24 MHz
  seg7_enable();     // enable 7-segment displays
  RTI_init();
  ix = 0;            // reset index into states
  dtime = 1;         // start display right away
  while(1) {         // do nothing while display goes
  }
}
```

Example 16

Circular Queue

In this example we will show how to create a circular character queue in C and how to use it in your main program.

16.1 A Circular Queue Data Structure

A circular queue is a useful data structure to use when you need to store characters read in an interrupt service routine. The queue can then be read as necessary without missing any of the received characters. In this example we will illustrate using a queue by storing values read from a keypad in a queue and then displaying them all on an LCD. In Example 17 we will use a queue to store characters received in the SCI port using interrupts.

A *circular queue* is shown in Figure 16.1. Multiple values can be stored in this queue before they are removed (in the same order they were stored). Therefore, characters will not be lost if they are received faster than they are removed. Of course, if the queue is full and another character is received, it will be lost. We will implement this queue in a separate C file called *queue.c* that is shown in Listing 16.1.

The queue is defined to be an array called *qbuff* containing *QMAX* bytes. The index of the first byte in the queue (0) is stored in the variable *min* and the index of the last byte in the queue (*QMAX*-1) is stored in the variable *max*. The index values *front* and *rear* are initialized to 0 in the C function *initq ()* in Listing 16.1 and serve as pointers to the front and rear of the queue. To store a value in the queue, the index *rear* is incremented and the value is stored at *qbuff[rear]*. However, when *rear* exceeds *max* it must wrap around to *min*. If *rear* ever runs into *front*, then the queue is full and we will back up *rear* and not store the new value. The complete algorithm for storing a value in the queue is

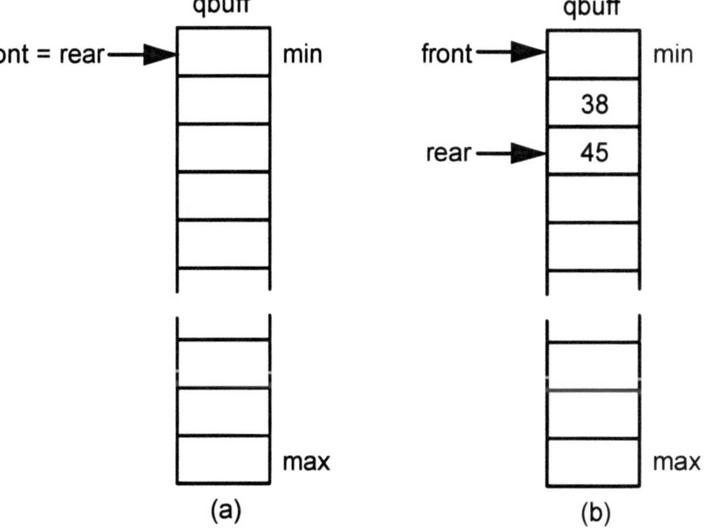

Figure 16.1 A circular queue:
(a) empty; (b) containing two values

implemented by the C function *qstore(char c)* in Listing 16.1 which stores the character *c* in the queue.

To read a value from the queue the index *front* is incremented and the value at *qbuff[front]* is read. This will guarantee that the first value stored in the queue will be the first one read from the queue. The queue will be empty any time that *front* = *rear*. The C function *int qempty(void)* shown in Listing 16.1 will return a 1 (true) if the queue is empty and return a 0 (false) if the queue is not empty.

Listing 16.1 A character queue (queue.c)

```
// queue.c  A character queue
#include  "queue.h"      // prototype definitions
#define   QMAX 16        // size of queue

static char qbuff[QMAX];  // the queue
static int  front;
static int  rear;         // queue pointers
static int  min = 0;      // start of queue
static int  max = QMAX-1; // end of queue

void initq(void){
       min = 0;
       front = 0;
       rear = 0;
       max = QMAX-1;
}

void  qstore(char c){
  rear++;                 // inc rear
  if(rear > max)
    rear = min;
  if(rear == front){
    rear--;               // queue is full
    if(rear < min)                   //  rewind rear
      rear = max;
  }else
    qbuff[rear] = c;                 // store c at rear
}

int qempty(void){
  int flag;
    if(front == rear)
      flag = 1;
    else
      flag = 0;
  return (flag);
}

char  getq(void){
  front++;                // inc front
  if(front > max)
    front = 0;
  return qbuff[front];    // return value at front
}
```

The variables in Listing 16.1 are defined to be static so they will not be visible to your main program *main.c*. To use this queue in your main program you will add the files queue.c (Listing 16.1) and queue.h shown in Listing 16.2 that is a header file containing the function prototypes. These will be available for you to use by including the statement *#include "queue.h"* in your main program as shown in Example 16 in Listing 16.3.

Listing 16.2 Function prototypes (queue.h)

```
// queue.h  A character queue
void  initq(void);        // initialize the queue
void  qstore(char);       // store character in queue
int   qempty(void);       // return 0 if queue is not empty
char  getq(void);         // read character from queue
```

Listing 16.3 Example 16

```
// Example 16: Example of using a queue
#include <hidef.h>              /* common defines and macros */
#include <mc9s12dg256.h>        /* derivative information */
#pragma LINK_INFO DERIVATIVE "mc9s12dg256b"

#include "queue.h"
#include "main_asm.h" /* interface to the assembly module */

void main(void) {
  char* blanks;
  char  c, a;
  blanks = "                ";

  PLL_init();                   // set system clock frequency to 24 MHz
  lcd_init();                   // enable lcd
  initq();                      // initialize the queue
  keypad_enable();              // enable keypad
  set_lcd_addr(0x00);           // display on 1st line
  while(1) {
    c = getkey();               // read keypad
    a = hex2asc(c);             // convert to ascii
    qstore(a);                  //   and store in queue
    data8(a);                   //   display on LCD
    wait_keyup();               //   wait to release key
    switch(c){
       case 0xE:                      // if enter (*) key
          set_lcd_addr(0x40);         // display on 2nd line
          while(qempty() != 1){       // empty the queue
             data8(getq());           //  and display on lcd
          }
          set_lcd_addr(0x00);         // clear 1st line
          type_lcd(blanks);
          wait_keyup();               // wait to release key
          set_lcd_addr(0x00);         // display on 1st line
          break;
       case 0xF:                      // if clear (#) key
          clear_lcd();                // clear lcd display
          wait_keyup();               // wait to release key
          break;
       default:
          break;
    }
  }
}
```

Example 17

SCI Receive Interrupts

In this example we will show how to use SCE receive interrupts and store the received characters in a queue.

17.1 SCI Interface Using Interrupts

In Example 8b we used the SCI port to receive characters typed on the PC keyboard and displayed the characters on the LCD. The problem with that example is that it takes some time to display a character on the LCD. If many characters are coming in the SCI port one after the other then some of the characters may be lost. This will happen if during the time it takes to write to the LCD and echo back the character one or more characters have overrun each other before they can be read using *inchar0()*. The solution to this problem is to enable receiver interrupts so that an SCI interrupt is generated each time a character is received. The interrupt service routine can then read the received byte and store the value in a queue using the function *qstore(char c)* as described in Example 16.

The built-in assembly language routines that can be used for SCI receive interrupts can be called using the C functions shown in Table 17.1. The functions for using the queue described in Example 16 are shown in Table 17.2.

Table 17.1 C Function calls for the SCI port with interrupts

Function	Description
`void SCI0_int_init(int b);`	Initialize SCI0 with interrupts and baud rate *b*
`char read_SCI0_Rx(void);`	Read character received in SCI0 Rx port
`void outchar0(char c);`	Output character *c* out SCI0 TxD pin
`void SCI1_int_init(int b);`	Initialize SCI1 with interrupts and baud rate *b*
`char read_SCI1_Rx(void);`	Read character received in SCI1 Rx port
`void outchar1(char c);`	Output character *c* out SCI1 TxD pin

Table 17.2 C Function calls for using the character queue in queue.c

Function	Description
`void initq(void);`	initialize the queue
`void qstore(char);`	store character in queue
`int qempty(void);`	return 0 if queue is not empty
`char getq(void);`	read character from queue

An example of using an SCI interrupt with a queue is given in Listing 17.1. Interrupt number 20 is the SCI0 interrupts and the function *SCI0_int_init(9600)* will enable receive interrupts and initialize the SCI0 port to 9600 baud. Every time a character is received the interrupt service routine *handler()* shown in Listing 17.1 will execute. This routine simply reads the received character using *read_SCI0_Rx()* and stores this value in the queue.

The main program continually monitors the queue and if there is a character in the queue it will read it (which removes it from the queue), write it to the LCD, and echo it back to the PC. Note that as long as the queue does not become full you will not miss any characters.

Test this program by downloading it to the miniDRAGON-Plus2 board and executing the program. Then close the download window so as to disconnect from the serial port. To make sure your program communicates properly, press the reset button, remove the serial cable from the miniDRAGON-Plus2 board, move the slide switch S7 to RUN, press the reset button, and replace the serial cable. If you are using a 20 x 4 LCD, run the program *host.exe* and download some text file that contains between 16 and 80 characters by pressing function key F6 and typing in the filename. Experiment by changing the size of the queue in *queue.c* so that you can display all 80 characters on the LCD.

Listing 17.1 Example 17

```
// Example 17: SCI using receive interrupts
#include <hidef.h>              /* common defines and macros */
#include <mc9s12dp256.h>        /* derivative information */
#include "queue.h"

#include "main_asm.h" /* interface to the assembly module */

#pragma LINK_INFO DERIVATIVE "mc9s12dp256b"

// SCI0 receive Interrupt Service Routine
void interrupt 20 handler(){
      qstore(read_SCI0_Rx());
}

void main(void) {
char c;
   PLL_init();            // set system clock frequency to 24 MHz
   lcd_init();              // enable lcd
   SCI0_int_init(9600);   // initialize SCI0 at with interrupts
   while(1){
     while(qempty() != 1){        // empty the queue
        c = getq();               //  and display on lcd
        data8(c);                 // write it to the LCD
        outchar0(c);              // echo it back
     }
   }
}
```

Example 18

Pulse Train Using Interrupts

In this example we will show how to generate a pulse train using an output compare interrupt on timer channel 6.

18.1 The HCS12 Timer Module – Output Compare

Timers are an important part of microcontroller interfacing. They can be used to produce delays, measure time intervals such as pulse widths, create various output waveforms such as pulse-width modulated signals, count the number of events, and other similar activities. We have already used the pulse-width modulation (PWM) module in Example 12 and the real-time interrupt in Example 14. The HCS12 family of microcontrollers has a fairly sophisticated timer subsystem associated with port T that can perform all of the above functions. All timer functions are based around a single, free-running 16-bit up counter called *TCNT*.

The two most basic functions that the timer can perform are output compares and input captures. We will use the output compare function in this example to generate a pulse train. In Example 19 we will use the input capture function to measure pulse widths and periods of input signals.

Each of the eight pins of port T can be programmed to output a pulse train using the output compare function. The way it works is that each pin has a 16-bit output compare register associated with it into which you can write a 16-bit value. When the free-running up counter, *TCNT*, reaches the value in the output compare register you can make any number of things happen. For example, you could have the pin go high, or go low, or toggle. You could cause an interrupt to occur on an output compare match in which you could update the output compare register for the next event you want to happen.

It turns out that pin 7 of port T (*PTT7*) is special in that it can be used in conjuction with any other pin to produce some useful effects. For example, suppose we want to produce the pulse train shown in Fig. 18.1. We can set it up so that on a *TC7* match (i.e. when the value of the free-running counter, *TCNT*, is equal to the contents of the output compare register, *TC7*) the signal on pin 6 will go high. We can also set it up so that on a *TC6* match (i.e. when the value of the free-running counter, *TCNT*, is equal to the contents of the output compare register, *TC6*) the signal on pin 6 will go low. If the value in *TC6* is *pwidth* greater than the value in *TC7* then the first pulse in Fig. 18.1 will occur when *TCNT* passes these two values. But how do we get it to produce the second pulse one period later? The answer is that we cause an interrupt to occur on the falling edge of the pulse train (i.e. on a *TC6* match) and in this interrupt service routine we will update the values of *TC6* and *TC7* based on the values of *pwidth* and *period.* The new value of *TC7* will be the old *TC7* plus *period* and the new value of *TC6* will be the new value of *TC7* plus *pwidth.* Note that it doesn't matter if these sums exceed 0xFFFF because the sum will simply wrap around as will the counter *TCNT.*

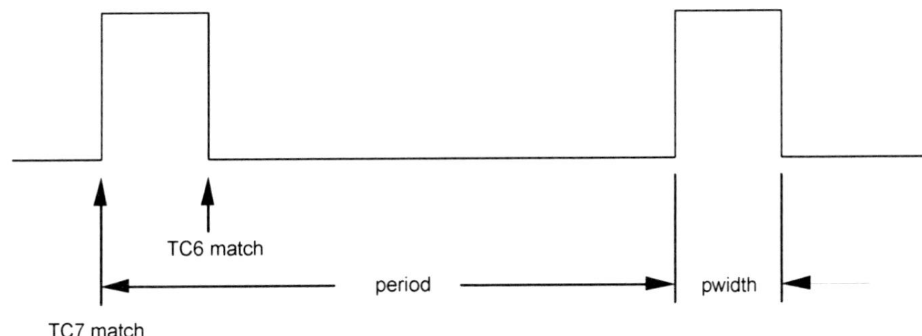

Figure 18.1 Pulse train

To make it easy we have written assembly language routines that can be called from the C functions shown in Table 18.1. The first two functions in Table 18.1 can be used to produce the pulse train in Fig. 18.1. An example of using these function calls to generate a pulse train on *PT6* is shown in Listing 18.1. Note that the timer clock is set to 1.5 MHz so that the largest possible period is 65,535/1.5 MHz = 43.7 ms.

Table 18.1 C Function calls for generating a pulse train

Function	Description
`void ptrain6_init(void);`	initialize pulse train interrupts on PT6 timer clock = 1.5 MHz
`void ptrain6(int period, int pwidth);`	update TC6 and TC7 in timer 6 interrupt routine
`void sound_init(void);`	initialize pulse train interrupts on PT5 (speaker) timer clock = 1.5 MHz
`void sound_on(void);`	Turn sound on by enabling timer and interrupts
`void sound_off(void);`	Turn sound off by disabling timer and interrupts
`void tone(int pitch);`	Set pitch value of sound by updating TC5 and TC7 in timer 5 interrupt routine

18.2 The miniDRAGON-Plus2 Speaker

The miniDRAGON-Plus2 speaker is connected to *PT5* by means of the jumper on header J10. (By moving this jumper you can connect the speaker to PP5.) We can produce sound by generating a square wave on *PT5* as shown in Fig. 18.2. We'll use the same interrupt scheme described above for producing the pulse train on PT6 shown in Fig. 18.1. The C function *sound_init()* given in Table 18.1 will initialize pulse train interrupts on *PT5* using a timer clock of 1.5 MHz. The C function *tone(pitch)* in Table 18.1 performs the same function as *ptrain(period, width)* by updating *TC5* and *TC7* in a timer 5 interrupt routine. The C functions *sound_on()* and *sound_off()* in Table 18.1 turn the sound on and off by enabling and disabling the timer and interrupts.

Listing 18.1 Example 18a

```
// Example 18a: Interrupt-Driven Pulse Train
#include <hidef.h>      /* common defines and macros */
#include <mc9s12dg256.h>     /* derivative information */
#pragma LINK_INFO DERIVATIVE "mc9s12dg256b"

#include "main_asm.h" /* interface to the assembly module */

int period;                    // period of pulse train
int pwidth;                    // high pulse width of pulse train

//  Timer channel 6 interrupt service routine
void interrupt 14 handler(){
    ptrain6(period, pwidth);
}

void main(void) {
  PLL_init();            // set system clock frequency to 24 MHz
  ptrain6_init();
  period = 5734;
  pwidth = 2867;
  while(1) {             // do nothing while generating pulse train
  }
}
```

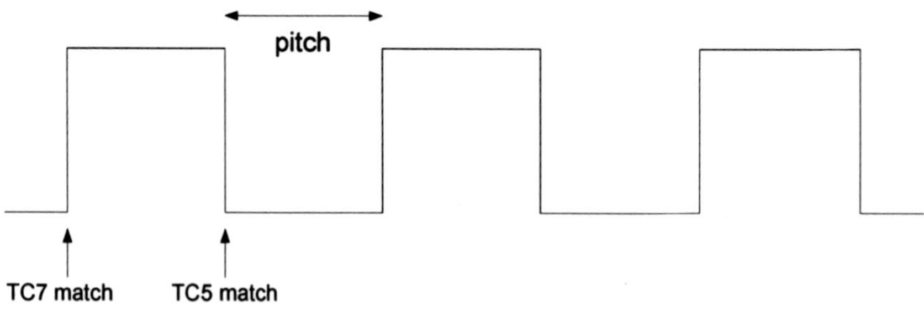

Figure 18.2 Square wave used to generate sound

The pitch values for different notes in the musical scale are shown in Table 18.2. Listing 18.2 is a C program that will play two octives of the musical scale when you press keys on a hex keypad starting on the lower left of the keypad.

Table 18.2 Pitch values of musical scale

Note	Freq (HZ)	Period (ms)	Pitch
Middle C	261.63	3.822	2867
C# D^b	277.18	3.608	2706
D	293.66	3.405	2554
D# E^b	311.13	3.214	2411
E	329.63	3.034	2276
F	349.23	2.863	2148
F# G^b	369.99	2.703	2028
G	392.00	2.551	1914
G# A^b	415.30	2.408	1806
A	440.00	2.273	1705
A# B^b	466.16	2.145	1609
B	493.88	2.025	1519
C	523.25	1.911	1434
C# D^b	554.37	1.804	1353
D	587.33	1.703	1277
D# E^b	622.25	1.607	1206
E	659.26	1.517	1138
F	698.46	1.432	1074
F# G^b	739.99	1.351	1014
G	783.99	1.276	957
G# A^b	830.61	1.204	903
A	880.00	1.136	853
A# B^b	932.33	1.073	805
B	987.77	1.012	760
C	1046.50	0.956	717

Listing 18.2 Example 18b

```
// Example 18b: Sound Example - play notes with keypad
#include <hidef.h>      /* common defines and macros */
#include <mc9s12dg256.h>     /* derivative information */
#pragma LINK_INFO DERIVATIVE "mc9s12dg256b"

#include "main_asm.h" /* interface to the assembly module */

// Define note, pitch, &  frequency.
#define  c     2867    // 261.63 Hz
#define  d     2554    // 293.66 Hz
#define  e     2276    // 329.63 Hz
#define  f     2148    // 349.23 Hz
#define  g     1914    // 392.00 Hz
#define  a     1705    // 440.00 Hz
#define  b     1519    // 493.88 Hz
#define  C     1434    // 523.25 Hz
#define  D     1277    // 587.33 Hz
#define  E     1138    // 659.26 Hz
#define  F     1074    // 698.46 Hz
#define  G     957     // 783.99 Hz
#define  A     853     // 880.00 Hz
#define  B     760     // 987.77 Hz
#define  CC    717     // 1046.50 Hz
#define  DD    639     // 1174.66 Hz

char k;
int pitch;
int pitchval[16] = {
  d, A, B, CC, D, E, F, g, a, b, DD, G, C, f, c, e
};
char * pitchdisp[16] = {
  "d", "A", "B", "CC", "D", "E", "F", "g",
  "a", "b", "DD", "G", "C", "f", "c", "e"
};

// Timer channel 5 interrupt service routine
void interrupt 13 handler(){
   tone(pitch);
   }

void main(void) {
 PLL_init();              // set system clock frequency to 24 MHz
 keypad_enable();               // enable the keypad
 lcd_init();                    // initialize LCD
 while(1){
   set_lcd_addr(0x00);          //set cursor to first line
   k = getkey();                //get keypad button pressed
   type_lcd(pitchdisp[k]);      //display note on lcd
   pitch = pitchval[k];         //pitch value of button pressed
   sound_init();
   sound_on();                  // start playing the note
   wait_keyup();                //wait for button to be released
   sound_off();                 // stop playing the note
   clear_lcd();
 }
}
```

Example 19

Measuring Pulse Widths Using Interrupts

In this example we will show how to measure the high time and low time (and therefore the period) of an input pulse train using an input capture interrupt on timer channel 1.

19.1 The HCS12 Timer Module – Input Capture

In Example 18 we generated a pulse train using the output compare feature of the timer module. The *input capture* feature of the timer module allows you to capture the value of the free-running counter, *TCNT*, into the input capture register, *TCx*, when a rising or falling edge (or both) occurs on the associated input pin *PTTx*.

The C function calls in Table 19.1 are to assembly language routines that will allow you to measure both the high and low times of an input pulse train on pin *PTT1*. The function *HILO1_init()* will enable TC1 interrupts on both edges of the pulse train. The timer clock is set to 1.5 MHz so that the maximum high or low pulse width that can be measured is 65,535/1.5 MHz = 43.7 ms.

The function *HILOtimes1()* is called in your interrupt service routine. It remembers the value of *TC1* that was read at the last interrupt and subtracts this value from the current reading of *TC1* to get the pulse width. It reads pin *PTT1* to see if the interrupt occurred on a rising edge (in which case the measured pulse width is low) or on a falling edge (in which case the measured pulse width is high). This function saves the most recent readings in two assembly language variables. You can get these values from your C program by calling the two functions *get_HItime1()* and *get_LOtime1()*.

Table 19.1 C Function calls for measuring pulse widths on Channel 1

Function	Description
`void HILO1_init(void);`	initialize input capture interrupts on both edges of channel 1 timer clock = 1.5 MHz
`void HILOtimes1(void);`	update HI – LO times in input capture interrupt routine
`int get_HItime1(void);`	return latest HI time of input pulse train
`int get_LOtime1(void);`	return latest LO time of input pulse train

Listing 19.1 shows an example of reading the high and low pulse widths of an input pulse train and displaying these values together with the period on the LCD display. Note that the values displayed will be multiples of 1/1.5 MHz = 0.667 μsec.

Listing 19.1 Example 19

```
// Example 19: Measuring Input Pulse Widths on Channel 1
#include <hidef.h>      /* common defines and macros */
#include <mc9s12dg256.h>     /* derivative information */
#pragma LINK_INFO DERIVATIVE "mc9s12dg256b"

#include "main_asm.h" /* interface to the assembly module */

//  Timer channel 1 interrupt service routine
void interrupt 9 handler1(){
    HILOtimes1();     // update HI-LO times on Ch 1
}

void main(void) {
  int period1;  // period of input pulse train on Ch 1
  int HI_time1; // measured HI time of pulse train on Ch 1
  int LO_time1; // measured LO time of pulse train on Ch 1

  PLL_init();          // set system clock frequency to 24 MHz
  lcd_init();
  HILO1_init();
    while(1) {
       HI_time1 = get_HI_time1();  // read new HItime1
       LO_time1 = get_LO_time1();  // read new LOtime1
       set_lcd_addr(0x00);
       write_int_lcd(HI_time1);     // write HItime on row 1 of lcd
       write_int_lcd(LO_time1);     // write LOtime on row 1 of lcd
       period1 = HI_time1 + LO_time1;
       set_lcd_addr(0x40);
       write_int_lcd(period1);      // write period on row 2 of lcd
       ms_delay(100);
  }
}
```

Example 20

Using Accelerometers

In this example we will show how to use the A/D converter to read the values from an x-y-z accelerometer module.

20.1 Measuring Acceleration

It is easy to measure all three components of acceleration using low-cost x-y-z acceleration modules based on MEMS technology. Wytec provides a tiny board that contains the Kionix KXPS5-3157 x-y-z accelerometer. The board comes with a 6 foot ribbon cable that plugs into header J5 on the miniDRAGON-Plus2 board. This connects the x-, y-, and z-components from the accelerometer module to channels 0 – 2 of ATD1 respectively. Listing 20.1 shows a program that will allow you to test the accelerometer module by continuously displaying the x-, y-, and z-components of acceleration on the first row of the LCD. As you tilt the accelerometer module these values will change because you are measuring the acceleration of gravity. When the module is horizontal the z-value will be maximum (corresponding to 1 g) and will become minimum if you turn the module over (corresponding to -1 g). When the module is horizontal the x- and y-values are reading an acceleration value corresponding to 0 g. These values will increase or decrease as you tilt the module in one direction or another.

You should run this program and tilt the accelerometer until you understand what it is measuring. Try shaking the module to see what maximum (and minimum) accelerations you can detect.

20.2 Measuring the Coefficient of Static Friction

The accelerometer module can be used to measure the coefficient of static friction using the setup shown in Fig. 20.1. A small block is placed on a piece of poster board that is taped at one end to the table. The other end of the poster board is lifted up until the block just starts to slide down the inclined plane. If this occurs at an angle θ then the coefficient of static friction μ_s is given by

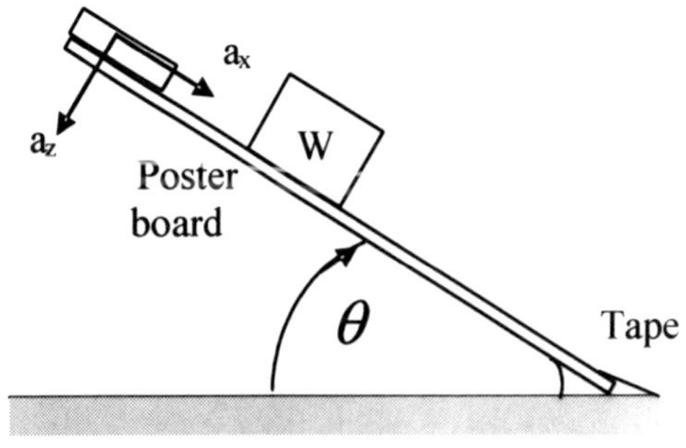

Figure 20.1 Measuring the coefficient of static friction

$$\mu_s = \tan\theta \qquad (20.1)$$

This result is easily derived by drawing a free-body diagram of the block.

The accelerometer is mounted on the poster board as shown in Fig. 20.1 where a_x and a_z measure the components of the acceleration of gravity, g. Thus,

$$a_x = g\sin\theta \qquad (20.2)$$

and

$$a_z = g\cos\theta \qquad (20.3)$$

From Eqs. (20.1) – (20.3) we see that

$$\mu_s = \tan\theta = \frac{a_x}{a_z} \qquad (20.4)$$

Listing 20.1 Example 20a

```
// Example 20a: Using accelerometer module: A/D Converter
#include <hidef.h>       /* common defines and macros */
#include <mc9s12dg256.h>     /* derivative information */
#pragma LINK_INFO DERIVATIVE "mc9s12dg256b"

#include "main_asm.h" /* interface to the assembly module */

int ax;
int ay;
int az;

void main(void) {
  PLL_init();          // set system clock frequency to 24 MHz
  ad1_enable();                  // enable a/d converter 1
  lcd_init();                    // enable lcd
  while(1) {
    set_lcd_addr(0x00);          // display on 1st row of LCD
    ax = ad1conv(0);             // read ax on channel 0
    write_int_lcd(ax);           // write value in field of 5
    ay = ad1conv(1);             // read ax on channel 1
    write_int_lcd(ay);           // write value in field of 5
    az = ad1conv(2);             // read ax on channel 2
    write_int_lcd(az);           // write value in field of 5
    ms_delay(100);               // delay 0.1 seconds
  }
}
```

To calculate the values of a_x and a_z to use in Eq. (20.4) we must subtract the value corresponding to zero gravity from the measured accelerometer values. Let a_0 be the measured accelerometer reading corresponding to zero gravity. We will assume that this value is the same value for both a_x and a_z. That is, it is the a_x value when $\theta = 0$, and is the a_z value when $\theta = 90^\circ$. We will measure a_0 by measuring a_x when $\theta = 0$. In order to deal only with integer values we multiply Eq. (20.4) by 1000 before doing the calculation. Thus, the integer that we compute will be calculated from

$$\mu_s = 1000\frac{a_x - a_0}{a_z - a_0} \qquad (20.5)$$

Listing 20.2 will perform this calculation.

Listing 20.2 Example 20b

```
// Example 20b: Calculating coefficient of static friction
#include <hidef.h>      /* common defines and macros */
#include <mc9s12dg256.h>     /* derivative information */
#pragma LINK_INFO DERIVATIVE "mc9s12dg256b"

#include "main_asm.h" /* interface to the assembly module */

int ax;
int az;
int a0;
int i;
long ax0;
long az0;
long tan_theta;

void main(void) {
  PLL_init();                // set system clock frequency to 24 MHz
  ad1_enable();                  // enable a/d converter 1
  lcd_init();                    // enable lcd
  a0 = 0;                        // average 8 values of ax to get a0
  for(i = 0; i < 8; i++){
    a0 += ad1conv(0);            // add 8 values of ax
  }
  a0 >>= 3;                      // divide by 8
  while(1) {
    ax = 0;
    az = 0;                      // average 8 values of ax and az
    for(i = 0; i < 8; i++){
      ax += ad1conv(0);          // add 8 values of ax
      az += ad1conv(2);          // add 8 values of az
    }
    set_lcd_addr(0x00);              // display on 1st row of LCD
    ax >>= 3;                    // divide by 8
    az >>= 3;                    // divide by 8
    write_int_lcd(a0);       // write a0 in field of 5
    write_int_lcd(ax);       // write ax in field of 5
    write_int_lcd(az);       // write az in field of 5
   // calculate coeff of static friction
    ax0 = ax - a0;
    az0 = az - a0;
    tan_theta = 1000*ax0/az0;
    set_lcd_addr(0x40);              // display on 2nd row of LCD
    write_long_lcd(tan_theta);       // write value in field of 10
    ms_delay(100);                   // delay 0.1 seconds
  }
}
```

To make the measurement you would make sure that the poster board was horizontal and then press the reset button. This will start the program and calculate *a0* by averaging eight readings of *ax*. Then lift the poster board slowly. The value of $\tan\theta$ times 1000 will continuously be displayed on the LCD. This displayed value when the block just starts to slide down the poster board will be 1000 times the coefficient of static friction.

20.2 Sending Periodic Acceleration Measurements to Matlab

It is often useful to measure the acceleration at fixed time intervals (say every 10 ms) and send this data to a Matlab program for further analysis. Listing 20.3 shows a program that will do this.

Listing 20.3 Example 20c

```
// Example 20c: Read all three acceleration channels every 10 ms
// and send the data to MATLAB
#include <hidef.h>      /* common defines and macros */
#include <mc9s12dg256.h>     /* derivative information */
#pragma LINK_INFO DERIVATIVE "mc9s12dg256b"

#include "main_asm.h" /* interface to the assembly module */

#define BufMax 1024     // size of buffer arrays (~10s/10.24ms)
int ax[BufMax];
int ay[BufMax];
int az[BufMax];
int count;
int reading;

void interrupt 7 handler(){  // RTI service routine
  if (count<BufMax && reading==1) {
    ax[count]=ad1conv(0);  // ax: channel 0
    ay[count]=ad1conv(1);  // ay: channel 1
    az[count]=ad1conv(2);  // az: channel 2
    count++;
  }
  clear_RTI_flag();
}


void main(void) {
  int i;
  char* message;
  int lsb,msb,al,ah;

  PLL_init();               // set system clock frequency to 24 MHz
  ad1_enable();          // enable a/d converter 1
  lcd_init();            // enable lcd
  SCI0_init(9600);        // initialize SCI0 at 9600 baud
  SW_enable();           // enable switches
  RTI_init();            // enable RTI

  count=0;               // initialize count
  reading=0;             // read flag: false

  message="SW5: get data";
  set_lcd_addr(0x00);
  type_lcd(message);

  message="SW2: send data";
  set_lcd_addr(0x40);
  type_lcd(message);
```

Listing 20.3 (cont.) Example 20c

```
  while(1) {
     if(SW5_down()){
        //  collecting the acceleration data
        message = " Collecting data";
        set_lcd_addr(0x00);
        type_lcd(message);
        reading=1;                 // set read flag true
        while(SW5_down()){           // wait to release SW5
        }
        reading=0;                 // stop reading data
        set_lcd_addr(0x00);
        write_int_lcd(count);
        message=" values     ";
        type_lcd(message);
     }
     if(SW2_down()){
        // sending the acceleration data to MATLAB
        if (count>0){
          message=" Sending data...";
          set_lcd_addr(0x40);
          type_lcd(message);
          count--;               // make sure buffer has data
          lsb = count & 0x00FF;
          msb = count >>8;
          outchar0(lsb);         // send LSB of count
          outchar0(msb);         // send MSB of count
          for(i=0;i<count;i++){
            al = ax[i] & 0x00FF;
            ah = ax[i] >> 8;
            outchar0(al);              // send ax lo
            outchar0(ah);              // send ax hi
            al = ay[i] & 0x00FF;
            ah = ay[i] >> 8;
            outchar0(al);              // send ay lo
            outchar0(ah);              // send ay hi
            al = az[i] & 0x00FF;
            ah = az[i] >> 8;
            outchar0(al);              // send az lo
            outchar0(ah);              // send az hi
          }
          message="                ";
          set_lcd_addr(0x40);
          type_lcd(message);
          while(SW2_down()){           // wait to release SW2
          }
        }
        else {
          message="No data to send";
          set_lcd_addr(0x40);
          type_lcd(message);
          while(SW2_down()){           // wait to release SW2
          }
          message="                ";
          set_lcd_addr(0x40);
          type_lcd(message);
        }
     }
  }
}
```

The real-time interrupt service routine (see Example 14) will read the *x*-, *y*-, and *z*-acceleration values every 10.24 ms if the variable reading is set to 1 and the arrays defined for *ax*[*count*], *ay*[*count*], and *az*[*count*] are not full. The maximum buffer size is defined to be 1024 (about 10 seconds of data) at the beginning of the program. Note that the main program will collect acceleration data as long as you are holding down switch SW5.

Once you have collected the acceleration data you must make sure that the CodeWarrior Debug window is closed and then run the Matlab function dragon2matlab() shown in Listing 20.4. Press switch SW2 to send the data out the serial port to Matlab. This Matlab function will collect the acceleration data and plot it on a graph. An example in which the accelerometer was bounced three times is shown in Fig. 20.2.

Listing 20.4 Matlab program to collect acceleration data

```
function dragon2matlab()
% 1.  Complile and flash the program in Example 20c
% 2.  Run the program and close the CodeWarrior Debug window
% 3.  Press and hold pushbutton S1 to collect acceleration data
% 4.  Run the MATLAB function dragon2matlab()
% 5.  Press pushbutton S2 to send collected data
% dragon2matlab()

s = serial('COM1','BaudRate',9600,'DataBits',8);
fopen(s);  %opens the serial port
count = fread(s,1,'int16')          %get 16-bit integer
for i = 1:count                     %get acceleration data
    ax(i)=fread(s,1,'int16');
    ay(i)=fread(s,1,'int16');
    az(i)=fread(s,1,'int16');
end
fclose(s);
dt=0.01024;                       %data collected every 10.24 ms
for i=1:count
    t(i)=(i-1)*dt;
end
plot(t,ax,'-r', t, ay, '-g', t, az, '-b')
```

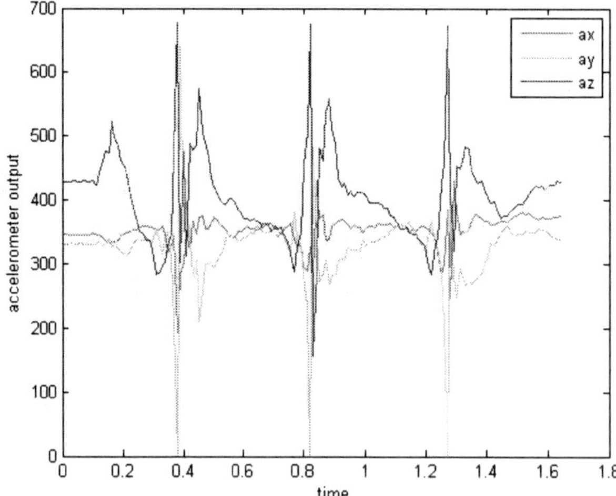

Figure 20.2 Matlab plot resulting from three bounces of the accelerometer

Example 21

Fuzzy Control

In this example we will show how to use the miniDRAGON-Plus2 board as a fuzzy controller. Before reading this example you should read Appendix E.

21.1 Design of a Fuzzy Controller

In Appendix E we show that the design of a fuzzy controller consists of the three parts shown in Fig. 21.1. The crisp inputs are first mapped to fuzzy sets using *get_inputs()*; the fuzzy rules are then applied to the input fuzzy sets using *fire_rules()*; and then a defuzzification operation is performed on the output fuzzy sets to produce a crisp output using *find_output()*.

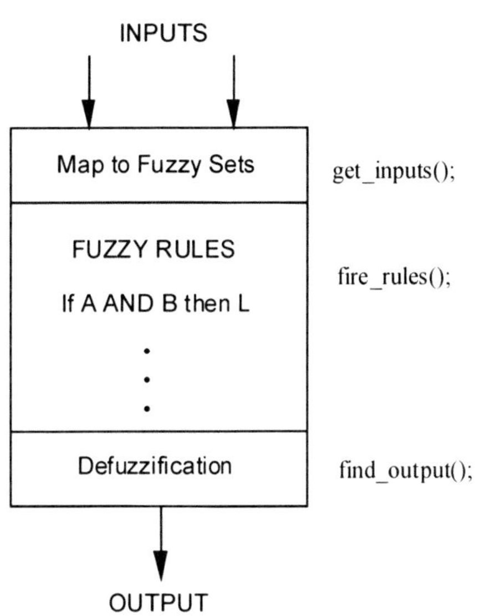

Figure 21.1 A fuzzy controller

In this example we will design a fuzzy controller that will keep a ping-pong ball floating at the center of a vertical, Plexiglas cylinder. The position of the ball could be measured using an ultrasonic transducer at the bottom of the cylinder. Two consecutive position readings can be used to determine the instantaneous velocity of the ball. The output of the fuzzy controller will be a signal that will control the speed of a muffin fan at the bottom of the cylinder that blows air up the cylinder to keep the ping-pong ball at the desired height. A second ultrasonic transducer outside the cylinder could measure the height of your hand above the floor, and the fuzzy controller could make the ping-pong ball follow your hand!

The first step in the design is to define the membership functions for the inputs. The two inputs to the controller will be the *ball_position* and *ball_speed* and we will use the two sets of membership functions shown in Fig. 21.2. To use the built-in HCS12 fuzzy control assembly language instructions the values of *ball_position* and *ball_speed* must be an 8-bit number between 0 and 255.

The second step is to define the output motor power. The output membership functions are defined as singletons and are shown in Fig. 21.3. Again the value of *motor_power* must be between 0 and 255.

The third step is to determine the fuzzy rules. These will be common sense rules based on the two inputs, *ball_position* and *ball_speed*, and the output, *motor_power*. It is convenient to represent these rules in the form of a 5 x 5 fuzzy K-map of the form shown in Figure 21.4. The entries in this fuzzy K-map are the membership functions of the output, *motor_power*.

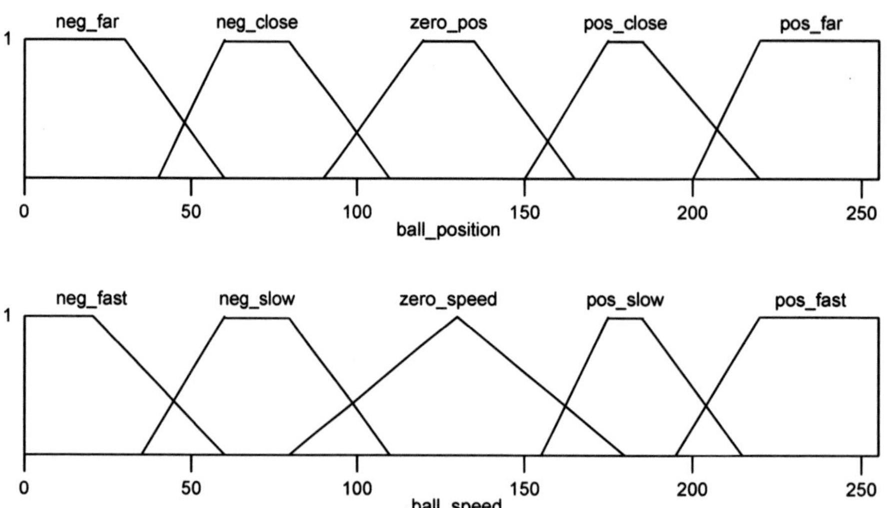

Figure 21.2 Input membership functions for floating ping-pong ball

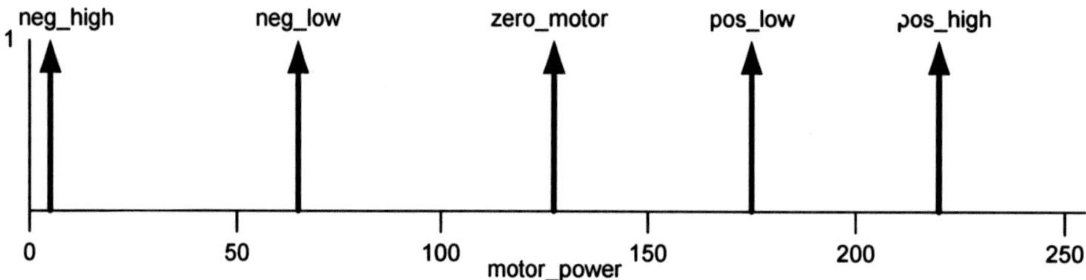

Figure 21.3 Output membership functions for floating ping-pong ball

For example, if the ball_position is *zero_p* (at its desired location) and the *ball_speed* is *zero_s* (it is not moving), then the change in *motor_power* should be *zero_m* (no change). This is the center entry in Figure 21.4.

If the *ball_speed* is *zero_s* (the center row in Figure 21.4) and the *ball_position* is *neg_close* (a little below the desired location) then we should increase the fan speed a little by setting *motor_power* to *pos_low*. If the *ball_position* is *neg_far* (a lot below the desired location) then we should increase the fan speed a lot by setting *motor_power* to *pos_high*. Similar arguments will hold if the *ball_position* is *pos_close* or *pos_far* leading to values of *motor_power* of *neg_low* (decrease fan speed a little) and *neg_high* (decrease fan speed a lot) respectively.

If the *ball_position* is *zero_p* (the center column in Figure 21.4) and the *ball_speed* is *neg_slow* (ball is falling slowly through the desired location) then we should increase the fan speed a little by setting *motor_power* to *pos_low*. If the *ball_speed* is *neg_fast* (ball is falling rapidly through the desired location) then we should increase the fan speed a lot by setting *motor_power* to *pos_high*. Similar arguments will hold if the *ball_speed* is *pos_slow* or *pos_fast* leading to values of *motor_power* of *neg_low* (decrease fan speed a little) and *neg_high* (decrease fan speed a lot) respectively.

		ball_position				
		neg_far	neg_close	zero_p	pos_close	pos_far
	pos_fast	zero_m	neg_low	neg_high	neg_high	neg_high
	pos_slow	pos_low	zero_m	neg_low	neg_high	neg_high
ball_speed	zero_s	pos_high	pos_low	zero_m	neg_low	neg_high
	neg_slow	pos_high	pos_high	pos_low	zero_m	neg_low
	neg_fast	pos_high	pos_high	pos_high	pos_low	zero_m

Figure 21.4 Fuzzy K-map for floating ping-pong ball

Similar arguments can be made for the four entries in each of the four corners of the fuzzy K-map in Figure 21.4. Note that the same fuzzy output membership function tends to occur on diagonal lines going from the upper-left to bottom-right of the diagram in Figure 21.4. This is typical of many fuzzy controller rules.

The HCS12 assembly language contains three sets of instructions that are useful for implementing a fuzzy controller. The *MEM* instruction will fill a *weights* array given an input and a set of membership functions. We will describe a C function call that uses this instruction in Section 21.2. The *REV* instruction is used to fire the rules. We will describe a C function call that uses this instruction in Section 21.3. The *WAV* instructions is used to calculate the output defuzzification centroid. We will describe a C function call that uses this instruction in Section 21.4.

21.2 Fuzzification of Inputs – MEM and *fill_weights()*

The first step in designing a fuzzy controller is to define the membership functions for all inputs and the output. Each membership function can be defined by the four parameters *u1*, *u2*, *u3*, and *u4* shown in Figure 21.5. The *MEM* instruction requires that the values *u1* and *u4* be 8-bit values between $00 and $FF. The weight values also range from $00 to $FF where $FF represents a weight value of 1.0 in Figure 21.5.

The *MEM* instruction does not use the parameters *u1*, *u2*, *u3*, and *u4* shown in Figure 21.5 to define the membership function. Rather it uses *u1* (called *point_1*) and *u4* (called *point_2*) together with the values of the two slopes, *slope_1* and *slope_2*, shown in Figure 21.5.

The value of *slope_1* is $FF/(*u2* - *u1*) and the value of *slope_2* is $FF/(*u4* - *u3*). These values can range from $01 to $FF. If u1 = u2 or u3 = u4 then the slope is really infinite. In this case the values of *slope_1* and/or *slope_2* are taken to be $00 inasmuch as this value is not used otherwise. A special case is a singleton, or "crisp" membership function. This can be defined by setting *u1* = *u4* and *slope_1* = *slope_2* = $00.

In the example program shown in Listing 21.1 we have allowed you to enter the membership functions for *ball_position* and *ball_speed* using the parameters *u1*, *u2*, *u3*, and *u4* from Fig. 21.5 in the arrays *ball_position[]* and *ball_speed[]*. The function *get_slopes(const unsigned char ball[],unsigned char memb[],int maxsize)* in Listing 21.1c will then fill the arrays *memb_pos*[20] and *memb_speed*[20] with the *point_1*, *point_2*, *slope_1*, and *slope_2* format used by the *MEM* instruction.

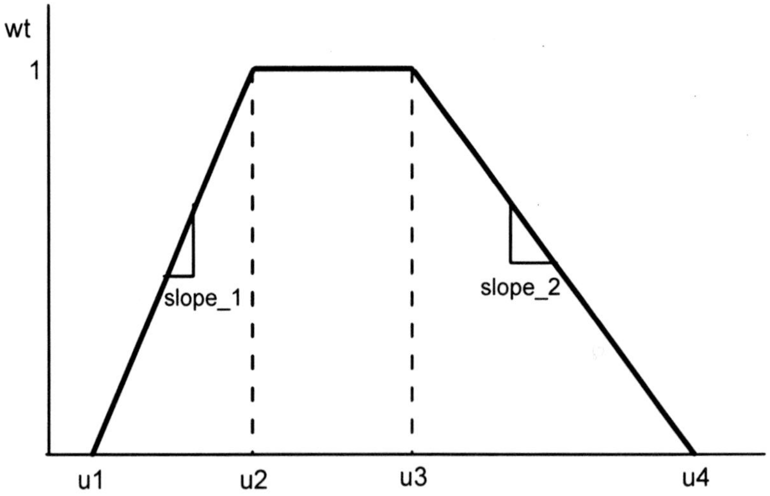

Figure 21.5 A membership function is defined in terms of u1, u2, u3, and u4

The *MEM* instruction requires accumulator *A* to contain the input value x_i and index register *X* to point to a data structure containing the two points and slopes that define the membership function as shown in Figure 21.6. Index register *Y* points to the element of the array *weight(j)* corresponding to membership function *j*.

The *MEM* instruction will compute the weight value at the input value x_i based on the membership function whose parameters are pointed to by *X*. The computed weight value ($00-$FF) is stored in the byte pointed to by *Y*. After the *MEM* instruction is executed *X* will have been incremented by 4 and *Y* will have been incremented by 1. If the four parameters of all membership functions for a single input are stored in adjacent bytes of memory, then *X* will be pointing to the parameters of the next membership function. Similarly, *Y* will be pointing to the next element in the array *weight(j)*.

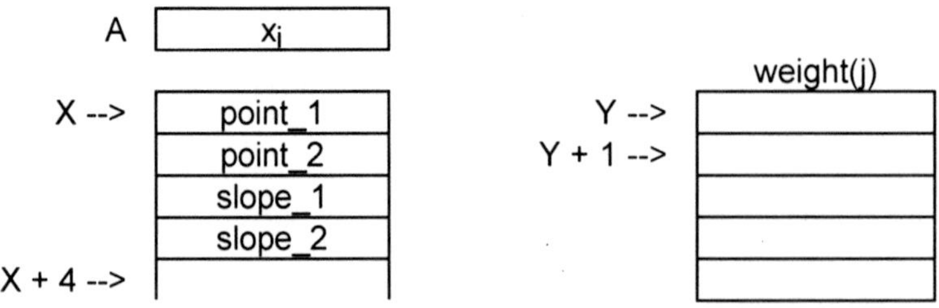

Figure 21.6 Data structure used by the HCS12 MEM instruction

Listing 21.1a Example 21

```
// Example 21:  Fuzzy Control -- ping-pong ball
#include <hidef.h>      /* common defines and macros */
#include <mc9s12dg256.h>     /* derivative information */
#pragma LINK_INFO DERIVATIVE "mc9s12dg256b"

#include "main_asm.h" /* interface to the assembly module */

#define NUM_MEMB = 5;

void get_slopes(const unsigned char ball[],unsigned char memb[],int
num_memb);

/* global variables definitions */
static  int num_memb_pos = 5;
static  int num_memb_speed = 5;
static  int maxsize = 20;
static  int num_memb_motor = 5;
static  int num_rules = 25;

void main(void) {
  // input membership functions
  const unsigned char ball_position[] = {
      0,  0, 30, 60,          // neg_far
     40, 60, 80,110,          // neg_close
     90,120,135,165,          // zero_pos
    150,175,185,220,          // pos_close
    200,220,255,255           // pos_far
  };
  const unsigned char ball_speed[] = {
      0,  0, 20, 60,          // neg_fast
     35, 60, 80,110,          // neg_slow
     80,130,130,180,          // zero_speed
    155,175,185,215,          // pos_slow
    195,220,255,255           // pos_fast
  };
  unsigned char memb_pos[20];
  unsigned char memb_speed[20]
  ;
  // output membership functions
  unsigned char cent[] = {
    5,65,128,175,220
  };
  unsigned char inout_array[] = {
    0,  // weight_pos[]    0 neg_far
    0,  //                 1 neg_close
    0,  //                 2 zero_pos
    0,  //                 3 pos_close
    0,  //                 4 pos_far
    0,  // weight_speed[]  5 neg_fast
    0,  //                 6 neg_slow
    0,  //                 7 zero_speed
    0,  //                 8 pos_slow
    0,  //                 9 pos_fast
    0,  // out[]          10 neg_high
    0,  //                11 neg_low
    0,  //                12 zero_motor
    0,  //                13 pos_low
    0,  //                14 pos_high
  };
```

Listing 21.1b Example 21 (cont.)

```
unsigned char rules[] = {
    0,5,0xFE,14,0xFE,     // if x1 is neg_far && x2 is neg_fast then y is pos_high
    0,6,0xFE,14,0xFE,
    0,7,0xFE,14,0xFE,
    0,8,0xFE,13,0xFE,
    0,9,0xFE,12,0xFE,
    1,5,0xFE,14,0xFE,     // if x1 is neg_close && x2 is neg_fast then y is pos_high
    1,6,0xFE,14,0xFE,
    1,7,0xFE,13,0xFE,
    1,8,0xFE,12,0xFE,
    1,9,0xFE,11,0xFE,
    2,5,0xFE,14,0xFE,     // if x1 is zero_pos && x2 is neg_fast then y is pos_high
    2,6,0xFE,13,0xFE,
    2,7,0xFE,12,0xFE,
    2,8,0xFE,11,0xFE,
    2,9,0xFE,10,0xFE,
    3,5,0xFE,13,0xFE,     // if x1 is pos_close && x2 is neg_fast then y is pos_low
    3,6,0xFE,12,0xFE,
    3,7,0xFE,11,0xFE,
    3,8,0xFE,10,0xFE,
    3,9,0xFE,10,0xFE,
    4,5,0xFE,12,0xFE,     // if x1 is pos_far && x2 is neg_fast then y is zero_motor
    4,6,0xFE,11,0xFE,
    4,7,0xFE,10,0xFE,
    4,8,0xFE,10,0xFE,
    4,9,0xFE,10,0xFF
  };

  unsigned char* ptr_memb_pos;
  unsigned char* ptr_memb_speed;
  unsigned char* ptr_weight_pos;
  unsigned char* ptr_weight_speed;
  unsigned char* ptr_inout_array;
  unsigned char* ptr_out;
  unsigned char* ptr_rules;
  unsigned char* ptr_cent;
  unsigned char x1;                              // input x1
  unsigned char x2;                              // input x2
  unsigned char y;                               // output y

  ptr_memb_pos = memb_pos;
  ptr_memb_speed = memb_speed;
  ptr_weight_pos = inout_array;
  ptr_weight_speed = inout_array+num_memb_pos;
  ptr_inout_array = inout_array;
  ptr_out = inout_array+num_memb_pos+num_memb_speed;
  ptr_rules = rules;
  ptr_cent = cent;

  PLL_init();            // set system clock frequency to 24 MHz
  get_slopes(ball_position,memb_pos,maxsize);
  get_slopes(ball_speed,memb_speed,maxsize);
```

Listing 21.1c Example 21 (cont.)

```
  // The fuzzy controller
  while(1) {
  //  x1 = get_position();      // (user defined)
      x1 = 100;                 // test case -- remove
      fill_weights(ptr_weight_pos,ptr_memb_pos,num_memb_pos,x1);
  //  x2 = get_speed();         // (user defined)
      x2 = 150;                 // test case -- remove
      fill_weights(ptr_weight_speed,ptr_memb_speed,num_memb_speed,x2);
      fire_rules(ptr_inout_array,ptr_rules,ptr_out,num_memb_motor);
      y = calc_output(ptr_out,ptr_cent,num_memb_motor);
  //  adjust_motor(y):          // (user defined)
  }
}


void get_slopes(const unsigned char ball[],unsigned char memb[],int
maxsize) {
  int j;
  unsigned char diff;
  for(j = 0; j < maxsize; j=j+4){
    memb[j] = ball[j];                        // point_1
    memb[j+1] = ball[j+3];                    // point_2
    diff = (ball[j+1] - ball[j]);
    if(diff == 0)
        memb[j+2] = 0;
    else
        memb[j+2] = 255/diff;                 // slope_1
    diff = (ball[j+3] - ball[j+2]);
    if(diff == 0)
        memb[j+3] = 0;
    else
        memb[j+3] = 255/diff;                 // slope_2
  }
}
```

In Listing 21.1a we have included the three arrays *weight_pos[]*, *weight_speed[]*, and *out[]* in a single array called *inout_array[]*. The reason for doing this is that the *MEM* instruction requires that *weight_pos[]* and *weight_speed[]* be in consecutive memory locations and the definition of the fuzzy rules (described in the next section) requires the *out[]* array to follow the *weight_pos[]* and *weight_speed[]* arrays.

We have written an assembly language routine that is called by the C function *void **fill_weights**(unsigned char* weight, unsigned char* membx, int num_mem_fncs, char x)* that will call the *MEM* function *num_mem_fncs* times. This function will fuzzify the crisp input *x* by filling the weight array pointed to by *weight* with the appropriate weights based on the set of membership functions pointed to by *membx*.

21.3 Processing the Rules – REV and *fire_rules(...)*

We will use the MIN-MAX rule described in Appendix E to find the contribution of each rule to the output. The outputs are assumed to be represented by k singleton membership functions L^k. These membership functions are defined by the singleton centroids, $cent^k$. An output array, *out(k)*, will contain the maximum over all the rules of the minimum weights from all inputs. The purpose of the function *void* ***fire_rules****(unsigned char* inout_array, unsigned char* rules, unsigned char* out, int numout)* is to fill the elements of the output weight vector, *out(k)*. A fuzzy rule with two inputs can be represented by the triplet $(A^1_j, A^2_j; L_j)$ where the subscript j refers to the jth fuzzy rule. Let the value A^1_j be the address (pointer) of the kth element of the weight vector $weight_1(k)$ for input 1. A^1_j will therefore correspond to one of the membership functions (and therefore one of the fuzzy sets) of input 1. Similarly, A^2_j will be the address of the kth element of the weight vector $weight_2(k)$ for input 2. In general, A^i_j will be the address of the kth element of the weight vector $weight_i(k)$ for input i. The pseudocode for the function *fire_rules()* is given in Figure 21.7. We will next see how this pseudocode can be implemented using the HCS12 *REV* instruction.

```
fire_rules()
clear out array;
for j = 1, num_rules
    {
    min_wt = 1;
    for i = 1, num_inputs
        {
        wt = weighti[Aij]
        if wt < min_wt
            min_wt = wt;
        }
        out[Lj] = MAX(Out[Lj], min_wt);
    }
```

Figure 21.7 Pseudocode for *fire_rules()*

The HCS12 REV Instruction

The setup required for the 68HC12 *REV* instruction is shown in Figure 21.8. Index register *Y* points to an *inout_array* that contains the input *weight(j)* arrays and ends with the *out(k)* array described above. The elements of the *weight(j)* and *out(k)* arrays are assigned offsets (0 - 14) which represent the various membership functions such as *neg_far* and *pos_high* as shown in Figure 21.8 and Listing 21.1a.

The array labeled *rules* in Figure 21.8 contains a series of bytes, pointed to by index register *X*, that contains an encoding of all the rules. Each rule is of the form

if *x1* is *neg_far* and *x2* is *neg_fast* then *y* is *pos_high*

The offsets in the *inout_array* corresponding to *neg_far* (0) and *neg_fast* (5) are stored in the first two bytes. This is followed by a byte containing $FE which separates the input antecedents from the output consequents. The next byte contains 14, the offset of *pos_high* in the *inout_array*. This is followed by another $FE which separates the last consequent offset from the first antecedent offset of the next rule. A byte containing $FF marks the end of the rules. This rule encoding scheme will allow any number of inputs and any number of outputs.

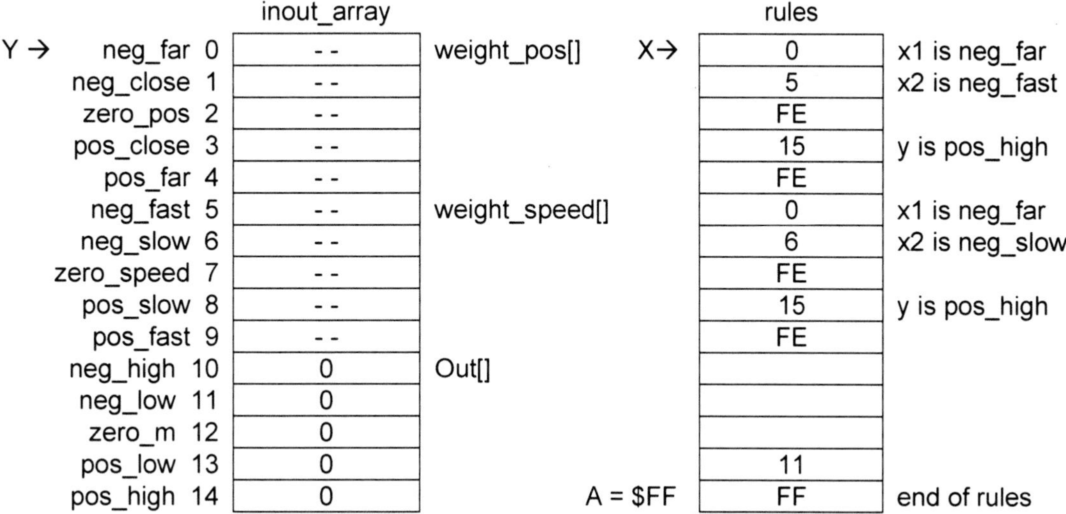

Figure 21.8 Setup required for REV instruction

The declaration of the *inout_array[]* is shown in Listing 21.1a and the definition of the complete *rule[]* array is shown in Listing 21.1b. The index numbers associated with each rule can easily be seen in Fig. 21.9 where we have redrawn the fuzzy K-map from Fig. 21.4 and included the corresponding index numbers from the *inout_array[]*.

		ball_position				
		neg_far 0	neg_close 1	zero_p 2	pos_close 3	pos_far 4
	pos_fast 9	zero_motor 12	neg_low 11	neg_high 10	neg_high 10	neg_high 10
	pos_slow 8	pos_low 13	zero_motor 12	neg_low 11	neg_high 10	neg_high 10
ball_speed	zero_speed 7	pos_high 14	pos_low 13	zero_motor 12	neg_low 11	neg_high 10
	neg_slow 6	pos_high 14	pos_high 14	pos_low 13	zero_motor 12	neg_low 11
	neg_fast 5	pos_high 14	pos_high 14	pos_high 14	pos_low 13	zero_motor 12

Figure 21.9 Fuzzy K-map inout_array[] indicies

In addition to initializing *X* and *Y* as shown in Figure 21.8, accumulator *A* must be set to $FF and the *out(k)* array must be initialized to zero before the *REV* instruction is executed. The *REV* instruction will then process all of the rules and fill the *out(k)* array following the pseudocode shown in Figure 21.7.

You may wonder how the *REV* instruction can tell the difference between the $FE at the end of the antecedents and the $FE at the end of the consequents. The answer is that it uses the overflow bit *V* in the condition code register as a flag to tell the difference. This bit is automatically set to zero when the statement *LDAA #$FF* is executed. The *REV* instruction then toggles this bit to 1 when it encounters the $FE at the end of the antecedents are clears it to zero by reloading accumulator *A* with $FF when it encounters the $FE at the end of the consequents.

The C function *fire_rules(...)*

We have written an assembly language routine that is called by the C function *void **fire_rules**(unsigned char* inout_array, unsigned char* rules, unsigned char* out, int numout)* that will first clear the out array. It then points to the *rules[]* array with index register *X* and to the *inout_array[]* with index register *Y*, sets accumulator *A* to $FF and calls the *REV* instruction. At this point the *out[]* array is filled with the appropriate output weights based on the entire list of fuzzy rules.

21.4 Output defuzzification – WAV and *calc_output(...)*

We will always use singleton fuzzy sets for the output represented by the centroids, $cent^k$. We will also use the MIN-MAX inference rule described in Appendix E. It should be clear from Figure E.11 in Appendix E that in this case the centroid y_0 will still be given by Eq. (E.11) where W^k is now the output array, *out(k)*, shown in Figure 21.8 and computed by the function *fire_rules(...)* described in the previous section.

Once the function *fire_rules(...)* has filled the output weight array *out(k)* the function *find_output(...)* will calculate the centroid y_0 using Eq. (E.11) in Appendix E. The pseudocode for the function *find_output(...)* is given in Figure 21.10. The centroids of the *Q* output membership functions are stored in the array $cent^k$.

```
find_output()
numer = 0;
denom = 0;
for k = 1, Q
   if out[k] != 0
      {
      numer = numer + out[k]*cent[k];
      denom = denom + out[k];
      }
y0 = numer/denom;
```

Figure 21.10 Pseudocode for *find_output(...)*

The HCS12 WAV Instruction

The values of *numer* and *denom* in Figure 21.10 can easily be calculated using the HCS12 *WAV* instruction. If index register *X* points to *cent[k]*, index register *Y* points to *out[k]*, and accumulator *B* contains the number of output membership functions, *Q*, then the HCS12 WAV instruction will compute a 24-bit value for *numer* and store the result in *Y:D* and compute a 16-bit value for *denom* and store this result in *X*. Therefore, if the

WAV instruction is followed by the instruction *EDIV* (see Appendix C) then the centroid value y_0 will be left in *Y*.

We have written an assembly language routine that is called by the C function *unsigned char* ***calc_output****(unsigned char* out, unsigned char* cent, int numout)* that will return the crisp output by using the WAV instruction as described above.

The complete while loop for the fuzzy controller is shown in Listing 21.1c. The functions *get_position()* and *get_speed()* are user-defined functions for reading the position and speed of the ping-pong ball. The position can be measured using an ultrasonic transducer. The speed can be computed by subtracting two successive position measurements.

After calling *fill_weights(...)* for both inputs, *fire_rules(...)*, and *calc_output(...)*, the word *adjust_motor(y)* is a user-defined word that will set the speed of the fan according the value of the output centroid *y*.

PROBLEMS

21.1 Run the program in Listing 21.1 using the simulator mode. Set a breakpoint at the first *get_slopes(...)* function and single-step through the instructions of each function call. Observe the contents of the *inout_array[]* and note how the output centroid value is calculated.

21.2

a. Implement the floating ping-pong ball fuzzy control problem described in this chapter. Use an ultrasonic transducer to measure the distance to the ping-pong ball. The difference between two consecutive distance measurements can be used to represent the ball speed. A muffin fan at the bottom of the Plexiglas cylinder is used to maintain the ping-pong ball at a fixed height within the cylinder.
b. Add a dial that you can use to set the height of the ping-pong ball.
c. Add a mode that has the ping-pong ball move between two different heights every 10 seconds.
d. Use a second ultrasonic transducer to measure the distance from the floor to your hand. Use the serial port to send this distance to your ping-pong ball setup. Have the ping-pong ball float at the height of your hand above the floor. As you move your hand up and down, the ping-pong ball should follow!

21.3 A fuzzy controller is used to maintain the idle speed of an automobile engine. The idle speed can be controlled by varying both the throttle position and the spark advance. In this problem we will consider only the throttle position. The two inputs will be

x1: the RPM error (current RPM - desired RPM)
x2: the change in RPM error from one measurement to the next

The output, *y*, will be a signal to a stepper motor that changes the throttle position. All input and output values are scaled from 0 - 255. The membership functions for the two inputs are given in the following tables.

Input x1	u1	u2	u3	u4
NM_1	0	0	20	100
NS_1	0	100	100	120
Z_1	100	128	128	156
PS_1	136	156	156	255
PM_1	156	235	255	255

Input x2	u1	u2	u3	u4
NS_2	0	0	64	128
Z_2	64	128	128	192
PS_2	128	192	255	255

The output, y, will have the five centroid values, 10, 80, 128, 176, and 245, corresponding to *NM_y*, *NS_y*, *Z_y*, *PS_y*, and *PM_y*.

a. Make plots of the membership functions for the two inputs, $x1$ and $x2$, and the output, y.
b. Make up a list of rules that seem sensible to you. For example, one rule might be

   IF $x1$ is *NS_1* and $x2$ is *Z_2* THEN y is *PS_y*

   Make a fuzzy K-map of your rule set similar to the one shown in Figure 21.9.
c. Write a fuzzy control program for this problem by following the format in Listing 21.1.

21.4 Suggest how you might design a fuzzy control system for each of the following applications:

a. An auto-focusing camera.
b. The braking system of a truck.
c. A washing machine
d. A rain-dependent variable-speed windshield wiper.
e. An electric oven.
f. Acceleration and deceleration control of a train.
g. A robot manipulator.
h. A laser tracking system.
i. A refrigerator
j. An air conditioner.

Appendix A

CodeWarrior Tutorial

Make sure that the directory *Program Files → Freescale → CW for HC12 V4.5 → Stationery → HCS12 → HCS12_Stationery* contains the project *LBE_miniDRAGON_Plus2*. This project is available on the website *www.lbebooks.com*.

In this tutorial you will execute all of the programs in Examples 1 – 4.

1 Start the program by double-clicking the CodeWarrior IDE (12) icon on the desktop.

2. Select *File →New...* Select *HCS12 Stationery*. Type *Examples1_4* for Project name.

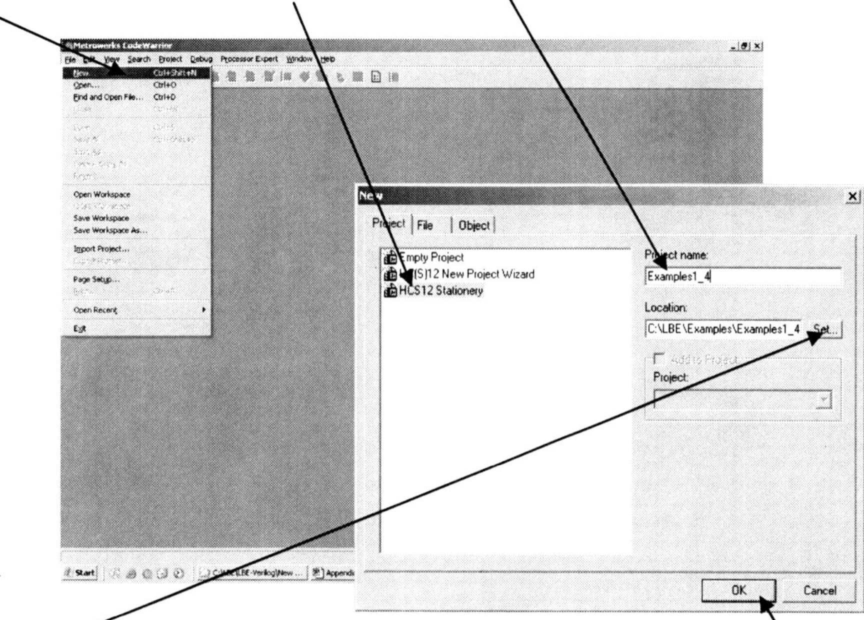

Set location where you want the project saved, and click *OK*.

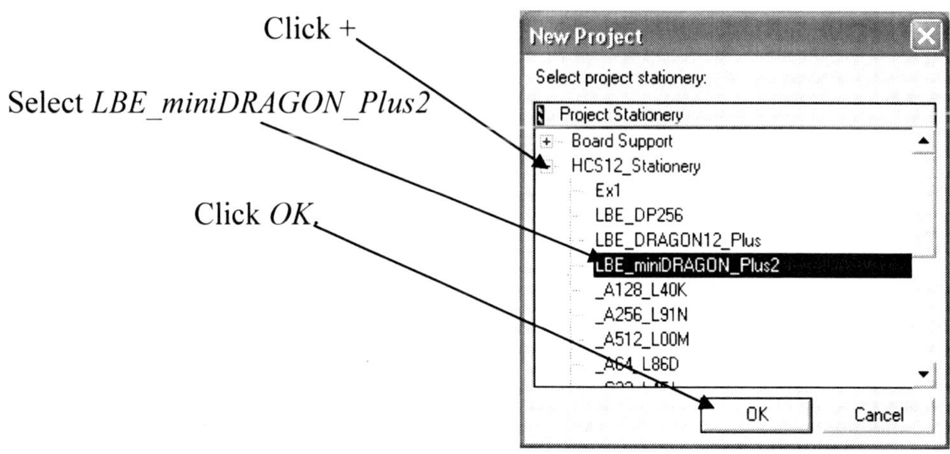

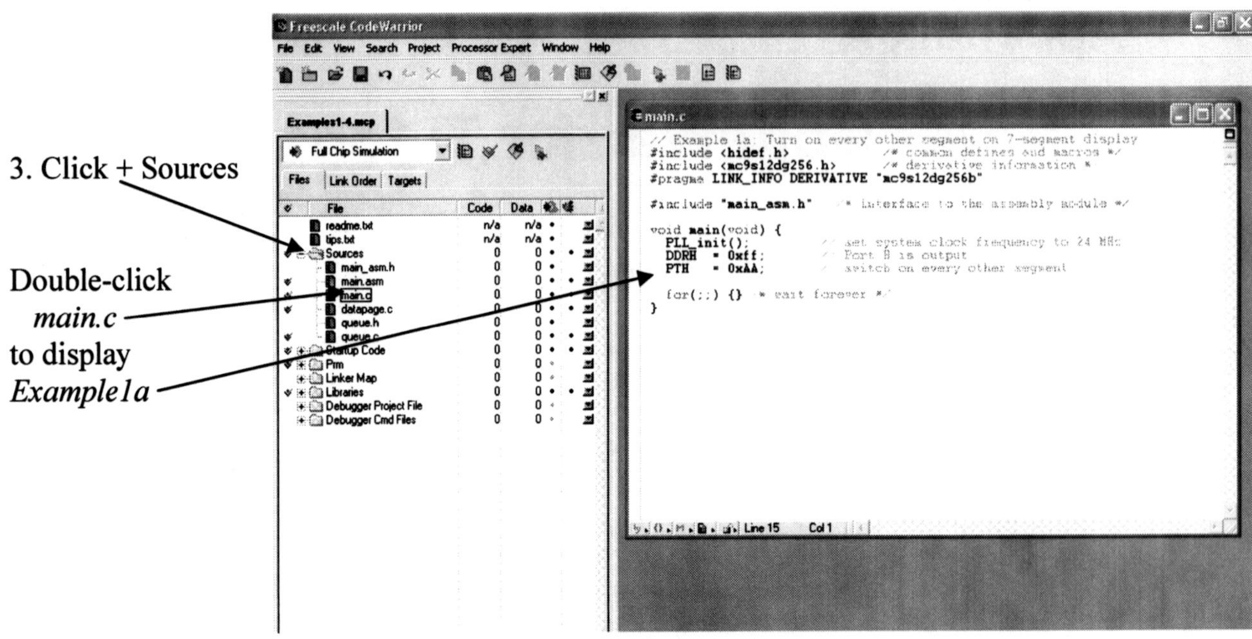

4. Make sure *HCS12 Serial Monitor* is selected. Click *Make* icon to compile program.

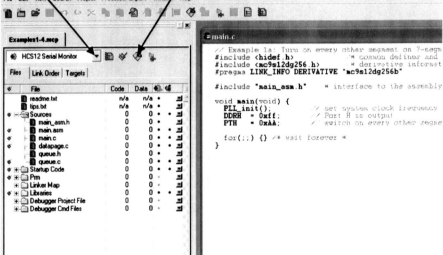

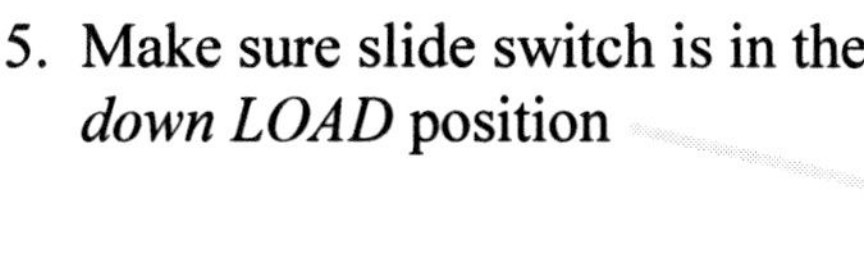

5. Make sure slide switch is in the *down LOAD* position

Make sure that the serial I/O cable is connected here

and the plug transformer is connected here

Then click *Debug* icon

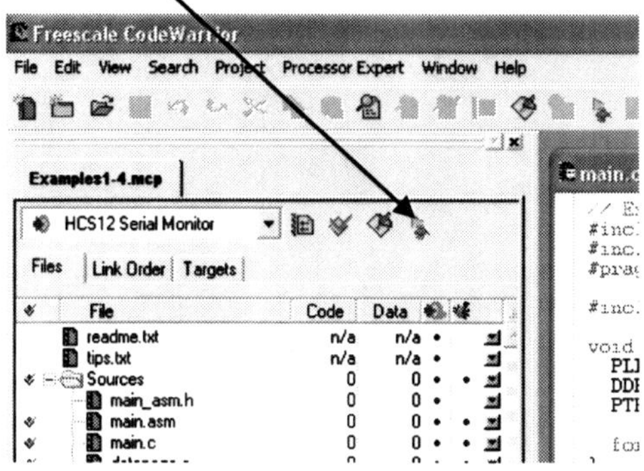

This will erase the flash memory (excluding the 2K bytes of protected flash containing the Serial Monitor) and bring up the following Debug window.

6. Click the *Start/Continue (F5)* icon to run the program.

Segments a, c, e, and g of the 7-segment display should be lit.

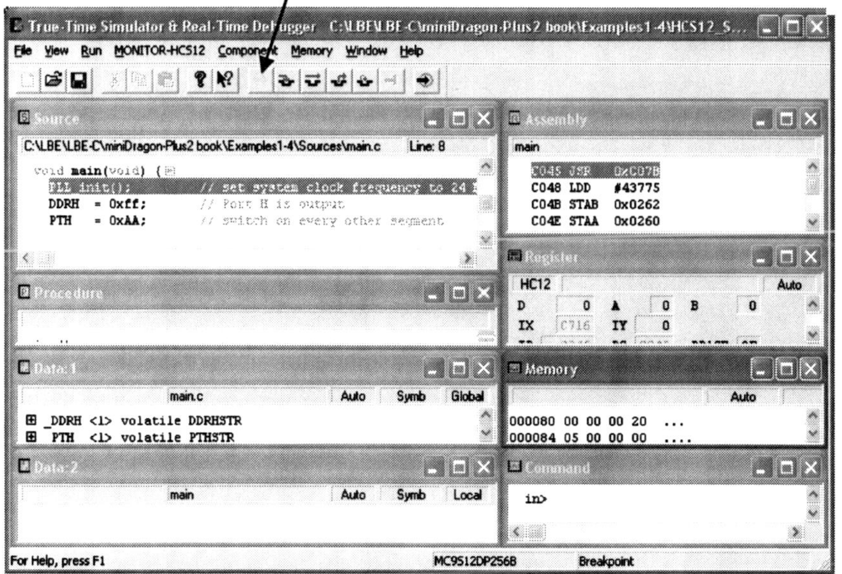

7. Press the reset button (the 7-segment display should go out)

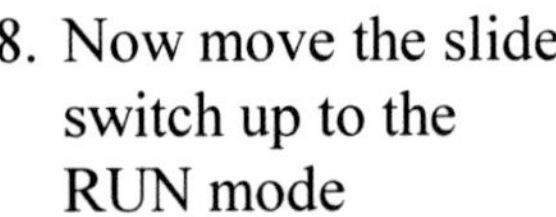

8. Now move the slide switch up to the RUN mode

9. Press the reset button again. Your program is running in flash memory on the board and the 7-segment display should come back on.

10. Now move the slide switch right back to the LOAD mod and press the reset button. Th Serial Monitor is running on board (the 7-segment display will go out) and you are ready to download a new program.

11. Close the Debug window

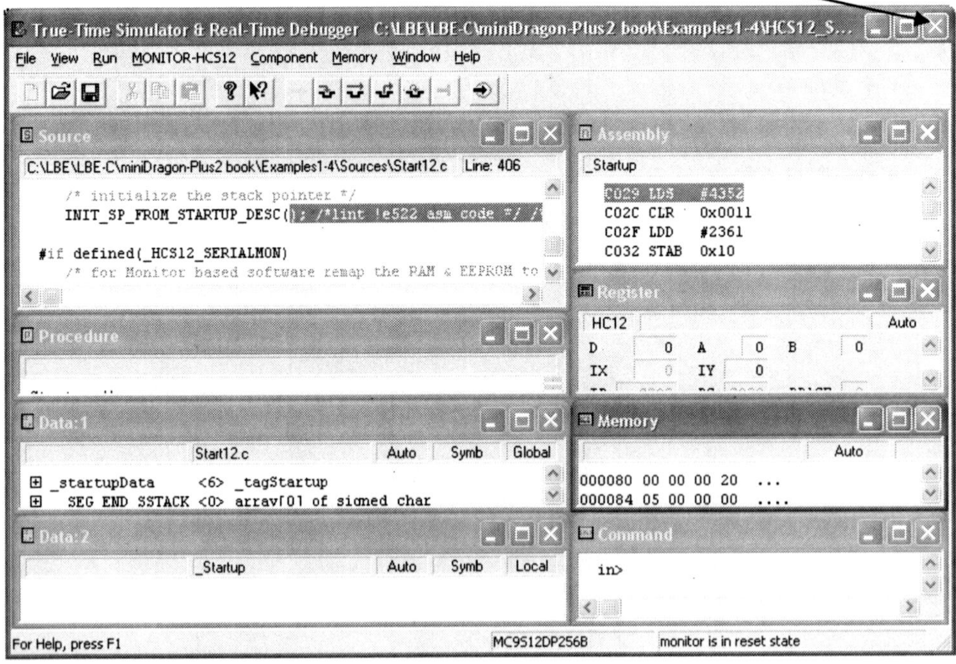

Example 1b – Read Example 1

At this point you could create a completely new project by following steps 2 and 3 above and edit *main.c* to be some new program. Instead we will keep the same project and just keep changing *main.c* to be Example1b – Example4b.

12. Select *File* → *Open…* Locate and open the file *Copy of Example 1b main.c*.

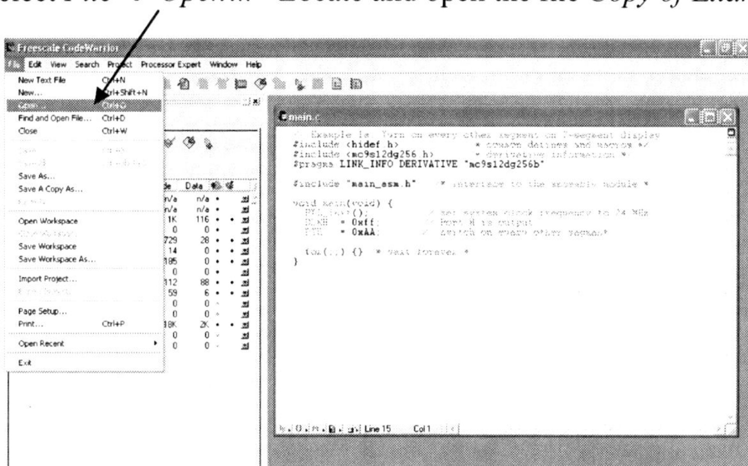

13. Select all of *Copy of Example 1b main.c* and copy it to the clipboard.

14. Select all of *main.c* and paste *Copy of Example 1b main.c* in its place

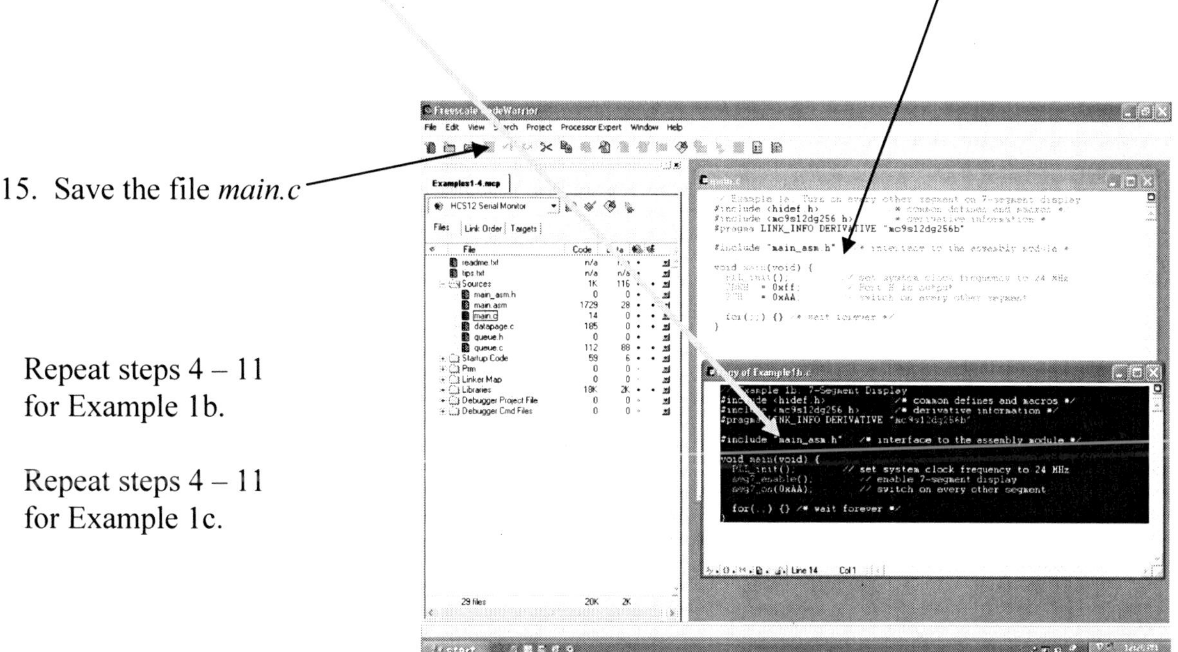

15. Save the file *main.c*

Repeat steps 4 – 11 for Example 1b.

Repeat steps 4 – 11 for Example 1c.

Read Example 2: Repeat steps 12 – 13 for *Copy of Example 2a main.c*.

Repeat steps 12 – 13 for *Copy of Example 2b main.c*.

Read Example 3: Repeat steps 12 – 13 for *Copy of Example 3a main.c*.

Repeat steps 12 – 13 for *Copy of Example 3b main.c*.

Read Example 4: Repeat steps 12 – 13 for *Copy of Example 4a main.c*.

Repeat steps 12 – 13 for *Copy of Example 4b main.c*.

Appendix B

HCS12 Assembly Language Essentials

B.1 The HCS12 Registers

The programming model of the HCS12 is identical with that of the 68HC11 and 68HC12. It consists of the set of registers shown in Figure B.1. We will refer to these as the CPU12 registers. The HCS12 also contains a register block that is associated with the various I/O operations of the HCS12.

In this section we will describe the CPU12 registers and illustrate how data can be moved into and out of these registers using some of the HCS12 instructions and addressing modes.

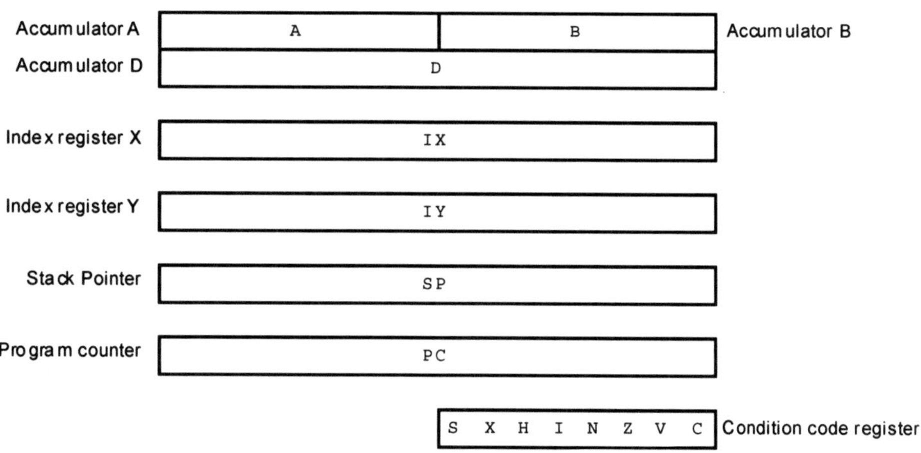

Figure B.1 The HCS12 Registers

B.1.1 The HCS12 Accumulators

The HCS12 has two 8-bit accumulators, *A* and *B*, that can be combined into the single 16-bit accumulator *D*. That is, *A* is the upper 8-bits of *D* and *B* is the lower 8-bits of *D*. The accumulators are used for storing intermediate results and for performing arithmetic and logical operations. The following are some of the instructions involving accumulators A, B, and D.

Load and Store Instructions:

LDAA	Load A from memory
LDAB	Load B from memory
LDD	Load D from memory
STAA	Store A to memory
STAB	Store B to memory
STD	Store D to memory

Transfer and Exchange Instructions:

TAB	Transfer A to B
TBA	Transfer B to A
EXG A,B	Exchange A and B

Addition and Subtraction Instructions:

ABA	Add B to A
ADDA	Add memory to A
ADDB	Add memory to B
ADCA	Add memory with carry to A
ADCB	Add memory with carry to B
ADDD	Add memory to D
SBA	Subtract B from A
SUBA	Subtract memory from A
SUBB	Subtract memory from B
SBCA	Subtract memory with borrow from A
SBCB	Subtract memory with borrow from B
SUBD	Subtract memory from D

Decrement and Increment Instructions:

DECA	Decrement A
DECB	Decrement B
INCA	Increment A
INCB	Increment B

Compare and Test Instructions:

CBA	Compare A to B
CMPA	Compare A to memory
CMPB	Compare B to memory
CPD	Compare D to memory
TSTA	Test A for zero or minus
TSTB	Test B for zero or minus

Boolean Logic Instructions:

ANDA	AND A with memory
ANDB	AND B with memory
EORA	Exclusive OR A with memory
EORB	Exclusive OR B with memory
ORAA	OR A with memory

ORAB	OR B with memory

Clear, Complement, and Negate Instructions:

CLRA	Clear A
CLRB	Clear B
COMA	One's complement A
COMB	One's complement B
NEGA	Two's complement A
NEGB	Two's complement B

Shift and Rotate Instructions:

LSLA	Logic shift left A
LSLB	Logic shift left B
LSLD	Logic shift left D
LSRA	Logic shift right A
LSRB	Logic shift right B
LSRD	Logic shift right D
ASLA	Arithmetic shift left A
ASLB	Arithmetic shift left B
ASLD	Arithmetic shift left D
ASRA	Arithmetic shift right A
ASRB	Arithmetic shift right B
ROLA	Rotate left A through carry
ROLB	Rotate left B through carry
RORA	Rotate right A through carry
RORB	Rotate right B through carry

Stacking Instructions:

PSHA	Push A
PSHB	Push B
PSHD	Push D
PULA	Pull A
PULB	Pull B
PULD	Pull D

Some of the instructions in the above list describe an operation involving a memory location. Where in memory the data resides is determined by the addressing mode. In general, several different addressing modes can be used with each memory access instruction. We will discuss addressing modes in more detail in Section B.2.

B.1.2 Index Registers, X and Y

The index registers *X* and *Y* are 16-bit registers that are used for several different purposes. They can be used in a manner similar to the accumulators for temporary storage when moving 16-bit data to and from memory. The following are some of the instructions involving index registers *X* and *Y*.

Load and Store Instructions:

LDX	Load X from memory
LDY	Load Y from memory
STX	Store X to memory
STY	Store Y to memory
LEAX	Load effective address into X
LEAY	Load effective address into Y

Transfer and Exchange Instructions:

EXG X,Y	Exchange X and Y
XGDX	Exchange D and X
XGDY	Exchange D and Y

Addition and Subtraction Instructions:

ABX	Add B to X
ABY	Add B to Y

Decrement and Increment Instructions:

DEX	Decrement X
DEY	Decrement Y
INX	Increment X
INY	Increment Y

Compare and Test Instructions:

CPX	Compare X to memory
CPY	Compare Y to memory

Stacking Instructions:

PSHX	Push X
PSHY	Push Y
PULX	Pull X
PULY	Pull Y

The main use of the index registers *X* and *Y* is in conjunction with various modes of addressing. An addressing mode is what specifies where a particular data item is to be found. For example, the instruction *LDAA #$10* is an example of the *immediate addressing mode*. This means that the data $10 immediately follows the opcode in memory. The $ sign means that 10 is a hexadecimal value. The # sign means that it is immediate addressing. One of the most important addressing modes associated with the index registers *X* and *Y* is indexed addressing. For example, the instruction

```
LDAA 0,X
```

means load into accumulator *A* the byte in memory at the address that is in index register *X*. We say that *X* is pointing to a byte in memory. The zero in the above instruction is a displacement that gets added to the value of *X*. For example, the instruction *LDD 4,X* will load two bytes of memory into accumulator *D* (*A:B*). The byte at address *X*+4 will be loaded into accumulator *A* and the byte at address *X*+5 will be loaded into accumulator *B*.

B.1.3 Stack Pointer, SP

The stack is a region of memory that is set aside for storing temporary data. The stack pointer, *SP*, is a 16-bit register that contains the address of the top of the stack. The stack is used by the HCS12 to save the return address when a subroutine is called. It is also used to save register values when an interrupt occurs.

The stack can be used to save the contents of registers *A*, *B*, *X*, and *Y* using the instructions *PSHA*, *PSHB*, *PSHX*, and *PSHY*. These values are removed from the stack using the instructions *PULA*, *PULB*, *PULX*, and *PULY*.

The following are some of the instructions involving the stack pointer, *SP*.

Load and Store Instructions:

LDS	Load SP from memory
STS	Store SP to memory
LEAS	Load effective address into SP

Transfer and Exchange Instructions:

TSX	Transfer SP to X
TSY	Transfer SP to Y
TXS	Transfer X to SP
TYS	Transfer Y to SP
EXG X,SP	Exchange X and SP

Decrement and Increment Instructions:

DES	Decrement SP
INS	Increment SP

Compare and Test Instructions:

CPS	Compare SP to memory
CPY	Compare Y to memory

B.1.4 Program Counter, PC

The program counter, *PC*, is a 16-bit register that contains the address of the next instruction to be executed. When an instruction is executed the program counter is automatically incremented the number of times needed to point to the next instruction. HCS12 instructions may be from one to six bytes long. Therefore, the program counter may be incremented by 1 to 6 depending upon the instruction being executed.

Some instructions cause the program counter to change to some new value rather than simply be incremented. These include the branching, jump, and subroutine instructions. We will discuss subroutines in Section B.3 and branching instructions in Section B.4.

B.1.5 The Condition Code Register

The HCS12 has a condition code register (CCR) that contains five status flags or condition codes and three control flags. The five status flags are the carry flag *(C)* , the zero flag (*Z*), the negative flag (*N*), the overflow flag (*V*), and the half carry flag (*H*). The three control flags are the interrupt mask flag (*I*), the X-interrupt mask flag (*X*), and the stop disable flag (*S*). Each flag is one bit in the condition code register. The location of each flag is shown in Figure B.2.

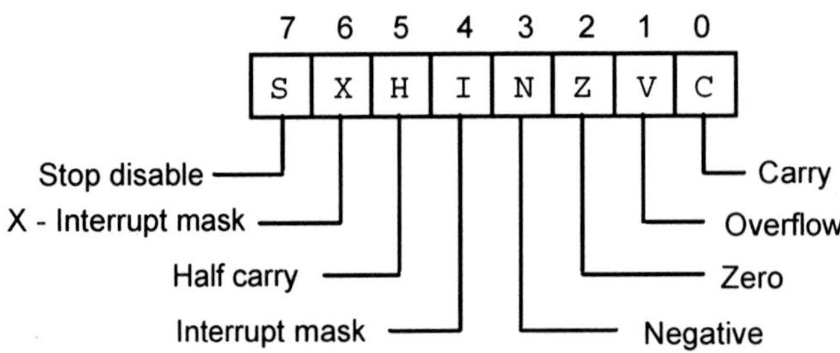

Figure B.2 The 68HC12 Condition Code Register

Any of the bits in the condition code register (with the exception of the *X* bit) can be set using the HCS12 instruction *ORCC*. This instruction will perform a logical OR of the CCR with a byte mask in memory (immediate addressing) containing a 1 in the bit locations to be set. Any of the bits in the condition code register can be cleared using the HCS12 instruction *ANDCC*. This instruction will perform a logical AND of the CCR with a byte mask in a memory containing a 0 in the bit locations to be cleared.

We will now look at the meaning of each bit in the condition code register.

Carry (C)

The carry flag is bit 0 of the condition code register. It can be considered to be an extension of a register, or memory location operated on by an instruction. The carry bit is changed by three different types of instructions. The first are arithmetic instructions. These include the addition instructions *ADDA*, *ADDB*, *ADDD*, *ADCA* (add with carry), *ADCB*, and *ABA* (add *B* to *A*), the subtraction instructions *SUBA*, *SUBB*, *SUBD*, *SBCA* (subtract with carry from *A*), *SBCB*, and *SBA* (subtract *B* from *A*), and the compare instructions *CMPA*, *CMPB*, *CBA*, *CPD*, *CPX*, and *CPY*. The carry bit is also changed by the multiplication instructions, *MUL*, *EMUL*, and *EMULS*, the five division instructions, *IDIV*, *IDIVS*, *EDIV*, *EDIVS*, and *FDIV*, the negate instructions, *NEG*, *NEGA*, and *NEGB*, and the decimal adjust instruction, *DAA*.

The second group of instructions that can change the carry bit are the shifting and rotating instructions such as *ASL*, *ASLA*, *ASLB*, *ASR*, *ASRA ASRB*, *LSL*, *LSLA*, *LSLB*, *LSR*, *LSRA*, *LSRB*, *LSRD*, *ROL*, *ROLA*, *ROLB*, *ROR*, *RORA*, and *RORB*.

Finally, the carry bit can be set to 1 with the instruction *SEC* (set carry), and cleared to zero with the instruction *CLC* (clear carry). These instructions which are valid for the 68HC11 get translated to the HCS12 instructions *ORCC #$01* and *ANDCC #$FE* respectively.

Zero Flag (Z)

The zero flag is bit 2 of the condition code register. This flag is set to 1 when the result of an instruction is zero. If the result of an instruction is not zero, the *Z* flag is cleared to zero. This *Z* flag is tested by the branching instruction *BEQ* (branch if equal to zero, *Z* = 1) and *BNE* (branch if not equal to zero, *Z* = 0). These branching instructions are described in Section B.4.

Negative Flag (N)

The negative flag is bit 3 of the condition code register. Negative numbers are stored in HCS12 computers using the two's complement representation. In this representation a negative number is indicated when bit 7 (the left-most bit) of a byte is set to 1. When the result of an instruction leaves the sign bit set (bit 7 of a byte or bit 15 of a word), the *N* flag is set to 1. If the result of an instruction is positive, (the sign bit is 0), the *N* flag is cleared to 0. The *N* flag is tested by the branching instruction *BMI* (branch if minus, *N* = 1) and *BPL* (branch if plus, *N* = 0). These branching instructions are described in Section B.4.

Overflow Flag (V)

The overflow flag is bit 1 of the condition code register. It is set any time the result of a signed (two's complement) operation is out of range. The *V* flag is tested by the branching instructions *BVS* (branch if overflow set, *V* = 1) and *BVC* (branch if overflow clear, *V* = 0).

Half Carry (H)

The half carry flag is bit 5 of the condition code register. It contains the carry from bit 3 to bit 4 resulting from an 8-bit addition or subtraction operation. The half carry flag is used by the microprocessor when performing binary-coded decimal (BCD) addition. As a programmer you normally don't need to worry about the half-carry flag.

Interrupt Mask Flag (I)

The interrupt mask flag is bit 4 of the condition code register. When it is set to 1, hardware interrupts are masked and the HCS12 will not respond to an interrupt. When the *I* flag is cleared to 0, interrupts are enabled and the HCS12 will service hardware interrupts.

The *I* flag is set to 1 with the instruction *SEI* (set interrupt mask) and is cleared to zero with the instruction *CLI* (clear interrupt mask). The 68HC12 translates these two instructions to *ORCC #$10* and *ANDCC #$EF* respectively. A more detailed discussion of interrupts will be given in Section B.5.

X-Interrupt Mask Flag (X)

The *X*-interrupt mask flag is bit 6 of the condition code register. This bit is set to 1 by a hardware reset at which point hardware interrupts entering the *XIRQ* pin of the microprocessor are masked. The *X* flag can be cleared to 0 with the instruction *ANDCC #$BF* after which *X*-interrupts are enabled. The 68HC11 can use to instruction TAP (which gets translated to *TFR A,CCR* in the HCS12) to clear the *X* flag. The *X*-interrupt mask can not be set by software. Therefore, once the *X* bit has been cleared to zero the *XIRQ* is essentially a non-maskable interrupt. A more detailed discussion of interrupts will be given in Section B.5.

Stop Disable Flag (S)

The stop disable flag is bit 7 of the condition code register. If this bit is set to 1 the STOP instruction is disabled. If this bit is cleared to 0 the STOP instruction is enabled. When this bit is set the STOP instruction is treated as a no operation (NOP) instruction. The STOP instruction is used to conserve power by stopping the internal clocks. An external interrupt is needed to start the clocks again.

B.3 Addressing Modes

Addressing modes determine the address where the data associated with instructions are located. This address is called the *effective address*. All of the HCS12 addressing modes are listed in Table B.1. Only the first six addressing modes in Table B.1 are available on the 68HC11. (On the 68HC11 the relative addressing and indexed addressing use only 8-bit offsets.)

The 68HC12 and HCS12 have added the seven new addressing modes shown in the bottom half of Table B.1. In addition, the 68HC12 and HCS12 allow 5-bit, 9-bit, and 16-bit constant offsets in the indexed addressing mode. The constant offset is added to *X*, *Y*, *SP*, or *PC* to compute the effective address. For example, if *X* contains the value $1234, then the instruction *LDD -2,X* will store the value in *D* at address $1234 minus 2 or $1232. This will store the contents of *A* at $1232 and the contents of *B* at $1233. Similarly, the instruction *JSR 0,Y* will jump to a subroutine at the address stored in *Y*.

The pre-decrement indexed addressing mode computes the effective address by first decrementing *X*, *Y*, or *SP* by a value of 1 to 8. For example, if *X* contains the value $1234 then the instruction *STAA 1,-X* will first decrement *X* by 1 to $1233 and then store the value of *A* at address $1233.

As a second example, consider the *MOVW* instruction which is of the form

```
MOVW   source,dest
```

and moves a word (16-bits) from the effective address *source* to the effective address *dest*. (There is also a *MOVB* instruction which moves an 8-bit byte.) The addressing mode for *source* can be either immediate, extended, or indexed, and the addressing mode for *dest* can be either extended or indexed.

For example, suppose that *X* contains the value $1234 and the word $5678 is stored at address $1234 as shown in Figure B.3. Then after executing the instruction *MOVW 0,X,2,-X* the value at address $1234 (0,*X*) will be copied to address $1232 (2,-*X*) and *X* will now be equal to $1232 as shown in Figure B.3.

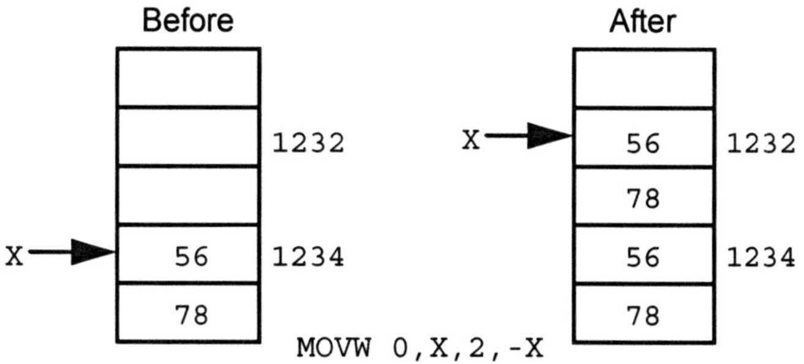

Figure B.3 Effect of executing the instruction *MOVW 0,X,2,-X*

Table B.1 HCS12 Addressing Modes

Addressing Mode	Description	Examples
Inherent	Data location is inherent in instruction	`INX` `DECB`
Immediate	Data immediately follows the opcode	`LDAA #$2C` `LDD #$1234`
Direct	Data is on page zero given by an 8-bit address ($00-$FF)	`STAA $FC` `STD $34`
Extended	Data is in memory given by a 16-bit address ($0000-$FFFF)	`STAB $1234` `STX $0848`
Relative	Opcode is followed by an 8-bit or 16-bit relative offset from PC	`BNE -$2B` `LBEQ $0452`
Indexed (constant offset)	5-bit, 9-bit, or 16-bit constant offset from X, Y, SP, or PC	`LDD -2,X` `JSR 0,Y`
Indexed (pre-decrement)	Auto pre-decrement X, Y, or SP by 1 - 8	`STAA 1,-X` `MOVW 0,X,2,-X`
Indexed (pre-increment)	Auto pre-increment X, Y, or SP by 1 - 8	`LDAB 1,+Y` `STD 2,+X`
Indexed (post-decrement)	Auto post-decrement X, Y, or SP by 1 - 8	`STD 2,X-` `LDAA 4,Y-`
Indexed (post-increment)	Auto post-increment X, Y, or SP by 1 - 8	`LDD 2,X+` `STAA 1,X+`
Indexed (accumulator offset)	Add contents of A, B, or D to X, Y, SP, or PC	`ADDA B,X` `STX D,Y`
Indexed-Indirect (16-bit offset)	Address of data located at 16-bit constant offset from X, Y, SP, or PC	`LDAA [0,Y]` `JSR [0,Y]`
Indexed-Indirect (D accumulator offset)	Address of data located at X, Y, SP, or PC plus the value in D	`ADDA [D,X]` `JSR [D,Y]`

The pre-increment indexed addressing mode computes the effective address by first incrementing *X*, *Y*, or *SP* by a value of 1 to 8. For example, if *Y* contains the value $1234 then the instruction *LDAB 1,+Y* will first increment *Y* by 1 to $1235 and then store the value of *B* at address $1235.

The post-decrement indexed addressing mode computes the effective address by using the value in *X*, *Y*, or *SP* (equivalent to *0,X*, for example) and then decrementing *X*, *Y*, or *SP* by a value of 1 to 8. For example, if *X* contains the value $1234 then the instruction *STD 2,X-* will store the value of *D* at address $1234 and then decrement *X* by 2 to $1232.

The post-increment indexed addressing mode computes the effective address by using the value in *X*, *Y*, or *SP* (equivalent to *0,X*, for example) and then incrementing *X*, *Y*, or *SP* by a value of 1 to 8. For example, if *X* contains the value $1234 then the instruction *LDD 2,X+* will load the value at address $1234 into *D* and then increment *X* by 2 to $1236.

The accumulator offset indexed addressing mode computes the effective address by adding the value of *A*, *B*, or *D* to *X*, *Y*, *SP*, or *PC*. For example, if *X* contains the value $1234 and *B* contains the value $12 then the instruction *ADDA B,X* will add the byte at address $1246 (*X*+*B*) to the value in *A* and leave the sum in *A*.

The 16-bit constant offset indexed indirect addressing mode adds a 16-bit constant offset to *X*, *Y*, *SP*, or *PC* to compute the address that contains the effective address. For example, if *Y* contains the value $1234 and if the value $5678 is stored at address $1234 then the instruction *LDAA [0,Y]* will load *A* with the byte at address $5678.

The *D* accumulator offset indexed indirect addressing mode adds the value in *D* to *X*, *Y*, *SP*, or *PC* to compute the address that contains the effective address. For example, consider the instruction *ADDA [D,X]*. If *X* contains the value $1234 and *D* contains the value $2345, then the value at $3579 ($1234+$2345) will contain the address of the byte that is added to accumulator *A*.

B.3 Subroutines and Stacks

B.3.1 The System Stack

The stack is a group of memory locations in which temporary data can be stored. A stack is different from any other collection of memory locations in that data is put on and taken from the *top* of the stack. The process is similar to stacking dinner plates on top of one another, where the last plate put on the stack is always the first one removed from it. We sometimes refer to this as a *last in-first out* or LIFO stack. In this section we will describe the HCS12 system stack.

The memory address corresponding to the top of the stack (the last full location) is stored in the stack pointer, *SP*. When data are put on the stack, the stack pointer is *decremented.* This means that the stack grows *backward* in memory. As data values are put on the stack they are put into memory locations with lower addresses. Data can be put on and taken off the stack using the *push* and *pull* instructions given in Table B.2.

When pushing one of the 8-bit registers, *A*, *B*, or *CCR*, on the stack the following operation takes place:

1) the stack pointer *SP* is decremented by 1.
2) the contents of the 8-bit register are stored at the address in *SP*.

When pushing one of the 16-bit registers, *D*, *X*, or *Y*, on the stack the following operation takes place:

1) the stack pointer *SP* is decremented by 2.
2) the contents of the 16-bit register are stored at the address in *SP*.
   (The high byte is stored at *SP* and the low byte is stored at *SP*+1.)

When pulling (sometimes referred to as popping) one of the 8-bit registers, *A*, *B*, or *CCR*, off the stack the following operation takes place:

1) the value at the address stored in *SP* is loaded into the 8-bit register.

2) the stack pointer is incremented by 1.

When pulling one of the 16-bit registers, *D*, *X*, or *Y*, off the stack the following operation takes place:

1) the value at the address stored in *SP* is loaded into the 16-bit register. (The byte at *SP* is loaded into the high byte and the byte at *SP*+1 is loaded into the low byte.)
2) the stack pointer is incremented by 2.

Table B.2 Push and Pull Instructions

Mnemonic	Function
PSHA	Push A
PSHB	Push B
PSHC	Push CCR
PSHD	Push D
PSHX	Push X
PSHY	Push Y
PULA	Pull A
PULB	Pull B
PULC	Pull C
PULD	Pull D
PULX	Pull X
PULY	Pull Y

As an example, suppose that the stack pointer, *SP*, contains the value $0A00 and the *D* register contains the value $1234. After executing the instruction *PSHD* the value $1234 will be stored at address $09FE as shown in Figure B.4. If the two instructions *PULB* and *PULA* are now executed in that order, then *B* will end up containing $12, *A* will end up containing $34 and the stack pointer, *SP*, will contain $0A00 again.

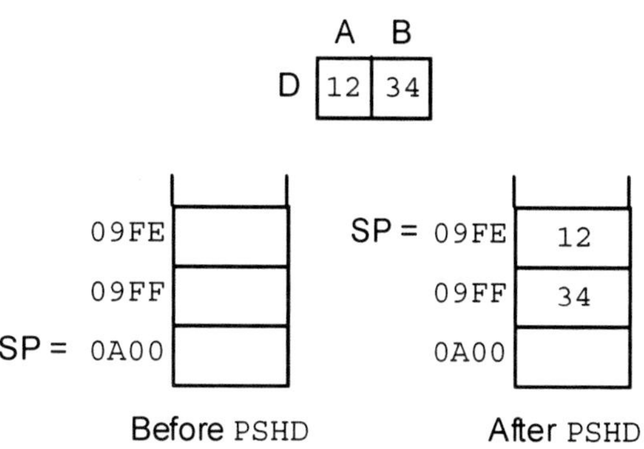

Figure B.4 Pushing D on the stack

B.3.2 Subroutines

A subroutine is a segment of code that is normally written to perform a particular function or task. A subroutine is called by executing a *JSR* (jump to subroutine) or *BSR* (branch to subroutine) instruction. A subroutine is exited by executing a *return from subroutine* (*RTS*) instruction. This will cause the program to return to the instruction following the *JSR* or *BSR* instruction that called the subroutine.*

The computer knows where to go when an *RTS* instruction is executed because it stored the return address on the stack when the *JSR* or *BSR* instruction was executed. The *RTS* instruction just pops the value on top of the stack into the program counter.

* The 68HC12 also has a CALL instruction that calls a subroutine in expanded memory. To return from such a subroutine one uses the RTC (return from call) instruction.

The *BSR* instruction uses relative addressing. It is a 2-byte instruction in which the second byte is a relative (two's complement) offset that gets added to the address of the next instruction to compute the subroutine address. This means that the address of the subroutine must be within ±128 bytes from the location of the *BSR* call. As a result the *BSR* instruction can only be used when calling nearby subroutines.

Several different addressing modes can be used with the *JSR* instruction. In the extended addressing mode the 16-bit address of the subroutine follows the opcode. For example, if in an assembly language program the label of a subroutine is *SUB1*, then the instruction *JSR SUB1* will be assembled using this extended addressing mode in which the address of *SUB1* will follow the *JSR* opcode.

As another example, if you want to jump to a subroutine whose address is in index register *Y*, you can execute the instruction *JSR 0,Y*. This is an indexed addressing mode in which the effective address is computed by adding a signed 5-bit offset (0 in this case) to the value in index register *Y*.

A program segment that calls a subroutine may be using a certain register, say *B*, for a particular purpose, such as a counter. If the subroutine changes the value of *B* then an error will occur in the calling program. To prevent this from happening a subroutine should save the values of registers that it modifies by pushing them on the stack at the beginning of the subroutine. Then they must be popped from the stack, in reverse order, at the end of the subroutine before the *RTS* instruction is executed. It is important to remember that the return address is on the stack and this is the address that is popped by the *RTS* instruction. Therefore, the same number of bytes must be popped from the stack at the end of a subroutine as were pushed onto the stack at the beginning of the subroutine. The structure of a typical subroutine is shown in Fig. B.5.

```
; subroutine example
subname
        pshb            ; save B
        pshx            ; save X
        ----
        ----            ; instructions that
        ----            ; change B and X
        ----
        ----
        pulx            ; restore X
        puxb            ; restore B
        rts
```

Figure B.5 Saving and restoring registers in a subroutine

B.4 Branching Instructions

The HCS12 has a large number of branch instructions. There are two major categories, short branch and long branch instructions. When writing assembly language programs you would normally use the short branch instructions. We will first look at short conditional branch instructions that test only a single bit in the condition code register. We will then explore the difference between unsigned and signed branch instructions.

B.4.1 Short Conditional Branch Instructions

The instructions shown in Table B.3 test the state of one of the flags in the condition code register. Other branching instructions, that will be described in later sections, test some combination of the status flags.

A branching instruction will cause a branch to occur if the branch test is *true*. For example, the branching instruction *BEQ* (branch if equal zero) will cause a branch in the program if the *Z* flag in the condition code register is 1. This will be the case if the result of the previous instruction produced a result of zero.

Table B.3 Simple Short Conditional Branch Instructions

Operation	Mnemonic	Branch Test
Branch if equal zero	BEQ	Z = 1
Branch if not equal zero	BNE	Z = 0
Branch if plus	BPL	N = 0
Branch if minus	BMI	N = 1
Branch if carry clear	BCC	C = 0
Branch if carry set	BCS	C = 1
Branch if overflow set	BVS	V = 1
Branch if overflow clear	BVC	V = 0

The conditional branch instructions shown in Table B.3 are all two bytes long. The first byte is the opcode and the second byte is the *relative displacement* of the branch destination. This is the two's complement number that must be added to the value of the program counter + 2 (the address of the next instruction) to obtain the address of the instruction to be executed if the branch test is *true*. If the branch test is *false*, then the instruction following the branch instruction is executed. This is illustrated in Fig. B.6. Note that if *Z* = 1 when the *BEQ* instruction is executed, the program will branch to the address formed by adding the displacement (06) to the address of the next instruction (5014); that is, to address 501A = 5014 + 06.

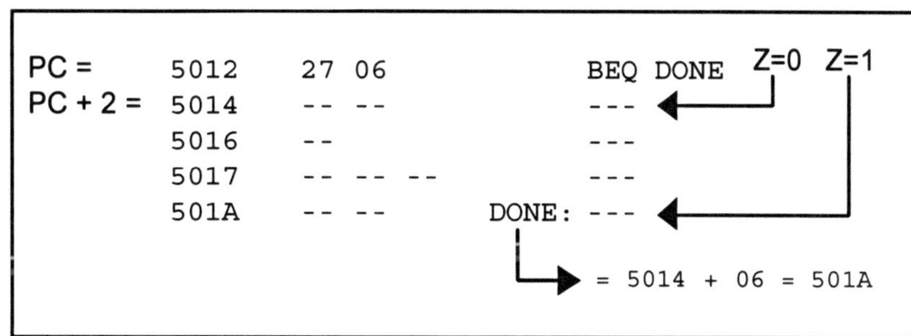

Figure B.6 The displacement (06) in a branch instruction is added to the program counter + 2 to obtain the destination address of the branch.

If a branching instruction branches backward in memory, the displacement must be negative. It is just the two's complement of the number of bytes between the address of the next instruction (*PC* + 2) and the branch destination address. These displacements are automatically calculated by the assembler.

As an example of calculating a branch displacement, suppose a branch instruction is to branch backward –8 bytes from the address of the next instruction. Since –8 is represented as a two's complement hexadecimal number by $F8, the branch displacement will be F8 as shown in Fig. B.7. Note that this subtraction is done by subtracting the address of the next instruction (*PC* + 2) from the destination address. The result, $FFF8, is the 16-bit hexadecimal representation of -8_{10}. When a two's complement, 8-bit hexadecimal number such as $F8 is stored as a 16-bit number, the sign bit (1 in this case) is extended to the left through the high order byte. Thus, $F8 and $FFF8 both represent the negative number -8_{10}. When using a short branch instruction, the displacement $F8 is used; when using a long branch instruction, the displacement $FFF8 is used.

```
            500C    --          LOOP1:  ---
            500D    -- --               ---
            500F    -- -- --            ---
PC =        5012    26 F8               BNE  LOOP1
PC + 2 =    5014    -- --               ---
            5016    -- -- --
                                    500C   LOOP1
                                   -5014   IP + 2
                                    FFF8
```

Figure B.7 Negative branches can be found by subtracting the address of the next instruction from the destination address

Note that since the branch displacement for the short branch instructions given in Table B.3 is a single 8-bit byte, a short branch instruction can only branch forward a maximum of 127 bytes ($7F) and backward a maximum of -128 bytes ($80). The counting of these bytes always begins at the address of the instruction *following* the branch instruction. At first this may seem like a serious limitation. Actually it is not. In fact, the 68HC11 has only short branch instructions. Well written assembly language programs should not need to branch conditionally more than ±127 bytes. Branches should take place within small program segments or subroutines. If you need to perform lots of instructions within a loop, for example, you should use subroutine calls to make the program more modular. This will make the program much easier to debug and maintain.

In the unlikely event that you do need to branch conditionally more than ±127 bytes you can use the HCS12 long branch instructions. Each of the instructions in Table B.3 has a long branch equivalent. For example, the instruction *LBEQ* (long branch if equal to zero) uses the test $Z = 1$ just as the instruction *BEQ* does. However, this instruction uses a 16-bit signed displacement rather than an 8-bit displacement. This means that the branching displacement can range from -32,769 ($8000) to +32,767 ($7FFF). The opcodes for the long branch instructions are two bytes long so that these long branch instructions use a total of four bytes and execute slower than the short branch instructions.

B.4.2 Unconditional Branch and Jump Instructions

The instructions in Table B.3 are *conditional* jump instructions that may or may not cause a branch to occur depending upon the value of one of the bits in the condition code register. Sometimes you may want to jump no matter what. This is called an unconditional branch or jump. Three different versions of unconditional branch and jump instructions are shown in Table B.4.

The short *BRA* (branch always) instruction has an 8-bit displacement as an operand. This is the same two's complement displacement described above for conditional branch instructions. It will allow an unconditional jump a maximum of 127 bytes forward or -128 bytes backward.

If you need to jump a farther distance you can use the long branch always instruction, *LBRA*. This requires a two-byte operand which represents a 16-bit two's complement number that must be added to the address of the next instruction to obtain the destination address.

Table B.4 Unconditional Branch and Jump Instructions

Operation	Mnemonic	Operand
Short Branch Always	BRA	8-bit displacement
Long Branch Always	LBRA	16-bit displacement
Jump	JMP	<effective address>

Both the short and long *branch always* instructions in Table B.4 use a *relative* displacement in the instruction. Since this is the number that is *added* to the address of the following instruction, it is independent of the destination offset address. This means that if the entire program is moved within the memory, this relative displacement does not change. The use of relative displacements for determining a destination address will allow you to write *position-independent code.* This means that a program can be moved to any location in memory and still run.

The *JMP* instruction shown in Table B.2 will jump uncondionally to the effective address determined by the particular addressing mode used in the operand. This could be an absolute address (extended addressing) or some form of indexed addressing.

B.4.4 Unsigned and Signed Branch Instructions

The conditional branch instructions given in Table B.3 are the ones most commonly used. In fact, you can write any program using only these. However, sometimes it is convenient to use the additional conditional branch instructions given in Tables B.5 and B.6. You must, however, be careful. It is very easy to make a mistake when using these conditional branch instructions. The instructions in Table B.5 must only be used when you are thinking about *unsigned* numbers; that is, 8-bit numbers with decimal values between 0 and 255 ($00-$FF), or 16-bit numbers with decimal values between 0 and 65,535 ($0000-$FFFF).

The branching instructions in Table B.6 must only be used when you are thinking about *signed* numbers; that is, 8-bit signed numbers with decimal values between –128

($80) and +127, ($7F), or 16-bit signed numbers with decimal values between –32,768 ($8000) and +32,767 ($7FFF).

Table B.5 Conditional Jump Instructions to Use Following a Comparison of UNSIGNED Numbers

Operation	Mnemonic	Branch Test
Branch if Higher	BHI	C **or** Z = 0
Branch if Lower or Same	BLS	C **or** Z = 1
Branch if Higher or Same	BHS	C = 0
Branch if Lower	BLO	C = 1

Table B.6 Conditional Jump Instructions to Use Following a Comparison of SIGNED Numbers

Operation	Mnemonic	Branch Test
Branch if Greater Than or equal	BGE	N **xor** V = 0
Branch if Less Than	BLT	N **xor** V = 1
Branch if Greater Than	BGT	Z **or** (N **xor** V) = 0
Branch if Less than or Equal	BLE	Z **or** (N **xor** V) = 1

It is very easy to confuse the instructions in Tables B.5 and B.6. This can lead to execution errors that are sometimes hard to find. For example, suppose accumulator *B* is used as a counter and you want to go through a loop 200_{10} ($C8) times. You might think that the loop shown in Fig. B.8 will work.

```
        CLRB             ;set B = 0
LOOP    INCB             ;increment B
        CMPB   #$C8      ;compare B to C8H
        BLT    LOOP      ;loop if B < 200
```

Figure B.8 How many times is the instruction INCB exectued?

It won't! The branching instruction *BLT LOOP* will fail the first time. This is because the value of *B* is 1 and the value of $C8 is not 200_{10} but is -56_{10}. Remember that the *BLT* instruction (and all the instructions in Table B.6) consider all numbers to be two's complement *signed* numbers. Inasmuch as 1 (the value of *B*) is greater than -56_{10} the instruction *BLT* will not branch.

The instruction you really want to use is *BLO* (branch if lower). This instruction, and all instructions in Table B.5 treat all numbers as unsigned numbers, so that $C8 is considered to be 200_{10} and not -56_{10}.

In Table B.5 note that the instructions *BHS* and *BLO* test only the carry flag and are the same as *BCC* and *BCS* respectively. All other instructions in Tables B.5 and B.6 use branch tests that involve more than one flag in the condition code register.

B.4.5 Bit-Condition Branch Instructions

The HCS12 has two bit-condition branch instructions that are given in Table B.7. The *BRCLR* instruction will branch if selected bits in a particular memory location are zero. The bits are selected by setting corresponding bits in a mask to 1. The *BRCLR* instruction will then branch if the logical AND of the memory location with the mask is zero. The general form of the instruction is

```
BRCLR  opr,msk,rel
```

where *opr* is the addressing mode for the memory location to be tested, *msk* is the mask value, and *rel* is the label of the branch destination address.

Table B.7 Bit-Condition Branch Instructions

Operation	Mnemonic	Branch Test
Branch if Selected Bits Clear	BRCLR	`(M) & (mask) = 0`
Branch if Selected Bits Set	BRSET	`!(M) & (mask) = 0`

The *BRSET* instruction shown in Table B.7 will branch if selected bits in a particular memory location are 1. In this case the *BRSET* instruction will branch if the logical AND of the one's complement of the memory location with the mask is zero.

B.4.6 Decrement and Branch Instructions

The HCS12 has two decrement and branch instructions that are given in Table B.8. The *DBEQ* instruction will decrement a counter (A, B, D, X, Y, or SP) and branch if the counter is equal to zero. The *DBNE* instruction will decrement a counter (A, B, D, X, Y, or SP) and branch if the counter is not equal to zero. As an example the instructions

```
fwl:        mem                 ; fuzzy membership grade
            dbne   B,fwl
```

are used in the fuzzy control function *fill_weights(...)* in *main.asm* to execute the *MEM* instruction B times.

Table B.8 Decrement and Branch Instructions

Operation	Mnemonic	Operation
Decrement counter and branch if = 0 (cntr = A, B, D, X, Y, or SP)	DBEQ	`cntr -1 -> cntr` `branch if cntr = 0`
Decrement counter and branch if not = 0 (cntr = A, B, D, X, Y, or SP)	DBNE	`cntr -1 -> cntr` `branch if cntr not = 0`

B.5 HCS12 Interrupts

There are over fifty sources of interrupts on the MC9S12DP256B as shown in Appendix D. These interrupts are divided into two categories: non-maskable and maskable. The maskable interrupts can be masked by setting the I-bit in the condition code register. Non-maskable interrupts cannot be masked. We will discuss non-maskable interrupt in Section B.5.1 and maskable interrupts in Section B.5.2.

B.5.1 HCS12 Non-Maskable Interrupts

There are six HCS12 non-maskable interrupts shown in Table B.9. Each interrupt source has a 16-bit vector address that holds the address (interrupt vector) of the code to be executed when the interrupt occurs.

Table B.9 HCS12 Non-Maskable Interrupts

Vector Address	Interrupt Source
`$FFFE-$FFFF`	Reset
`$FFFC-$FFFD`	COP Clock Monitor Fail Reset
`$FFFA-$FFFB`	COP Failure Reset
`$FFF8-$FFF9`	Unimplemented Instruction Trap
`$FFF6-$FFF7`	SWI
`$FFF4-$FFF5`	XIRQ

The non-maskable interrupts shown in Table B.9 are listed in order of priority. If more than one interrupt occurs at the same time, the interrupt with the highest priority will be serviced first. We will briefly describe each of these non-maskable interrupts in turn.

Reset

When the *RESET* pin on a HCS12 goes low, normal microprocessor functions are suspended. When this pin returns high the microprocessor will set bits *X* and *I* in the condition code register and start executing instructions starting at the address stored at $FFFE-$FFFF. The HCS12 has a power-on reset (POR) circuit that causes the reset signal to be asserted internally after power has been applied to the processor.

It is necessary for addresses $FFFE-$FFFF to be in some type of non-volatile memory (ROM, EPROM, or Flash memory) so that a valid reset vector will be at that address. Of course, the memory it points to must also be in non-volatile memory so that some meaningful code will be executed when you turn on the processor.

COP (Computer Operating Properly)

The two COP (computer operating properly) interrupt sources shown in Table B.9 are used to help detect both hardware and software errors. When the clock monitor is enabled (by setting the *CME* bit in the *COP Control Register*, *COPCTL*) special circuitry will produce a reset if the clock stops or its frequency falls below about 500 KHz.

The COP Failure Reset is a watchdog timer that will produce a reset if a special sequence ($55 followed by $AA) isn't written to the *Arm/Reset COP Timer Register* (*COPRST*) within a specified time. You would include this operation as part of your software when you know that certain portions of code must be executed within a certain time. A COP failure would be an indication that your software was not operating properly.

Unimplemented Instruction Trap

All 1-byte opcodes in the HCS12 are valid except $18 which requires a second byte to form the complete opcode. Only 54 of the 256 possible second bytes are valid. If your program tries to execute one of these invalid 2-byte opcodes, the program will trap to the address stored in $FFF8-$FFF9.

Software Interrupts (SWI)

A software interrupt occurs when you execute the *SWI* instruction. This will cause the instructions at the address stored in $FFF6-$FFF7 to be executed. Before this happens the return address (the address following the *SWI* instruction) is pushed on the stack together with registers *Y, X, A, B*, and *CCR* as shown in Fig. B.9. After pushing these values on the stack the interrupt mask, *I*, in the condition code register, *CCR*, is set to 1. This will prevent any maskable interrupts from being processed while in the software interrupt routine. The *I* bit can be cleared to zero by either executing the *CLI* (clear interrupt mask) instruction or by executing the *RTI* (return from interrupt) instruction. The *RTI* instruction is executed at the end of all interrupt service routines. It will pop from the stack all of the values shown in Figure B.9. This will include the *CCR* register which may have had the *I* bit cleared to zero if interrupts had been enabled before the *SWI* instruction was executed. A similar sequence occurs for maskable hardware interrupts which we will describe in Section B.5.2.

When the *RTI* instruction is executed the return address on the stack is popped into the program counter. The program will therefore continue at the point in the program where the interrupt occurred. For a software interrupt this would be the statement following the `SWI` instruction.

Non-maskable Interrupt Request (XIRQ)

The *XIRQ* is pin *PE0* on the HCS12. The *XIRQ* interrupt is a pseudo-non-maskable interrupt that is associated with the *X* bit in the *CCR*. After reset this bit is set which inhibits interrupts when the *XIRQ* pin goes low. However, software can clear the *X* bit in the *CCR* by using the instruction, *ANDCC #$BF*. Once this bit has been cleared it cannot be set to 1 again by software. Thus, at this point the interrupt becomes non-maskable.

When an *XIRQ* interrupt occurs by a high to low signal on pin *PE0* the current instruction is completed and then the registers shown in Figure B.9 are pushed on the stack. The return address will be the value in the program counter; i.e., the address of the instruction following the one being executed when the interrupt occurs. This will be the address returned to after the interrupt service routine is executed. The *XIRQ* interrupt service routine address is stored in the vector address $FFF4-$FFF5 (see Table B.9). After all registers shown in Fig. B.9 are pushed on the stack, both the *I* bit and the *X* bit in the *CCR* are set This means that another *XIRQ* interrupt cannot occur during the execution of an *XIRQ* interrupt service routine. Executing the *RTI* instruction at the end of the interrupt service routine will pop the registers shown in Figure B.9 off the stack, including the *CCR* register which will have its *X* bit cleared. At that point a new *XIRQ* interrupt can occur.

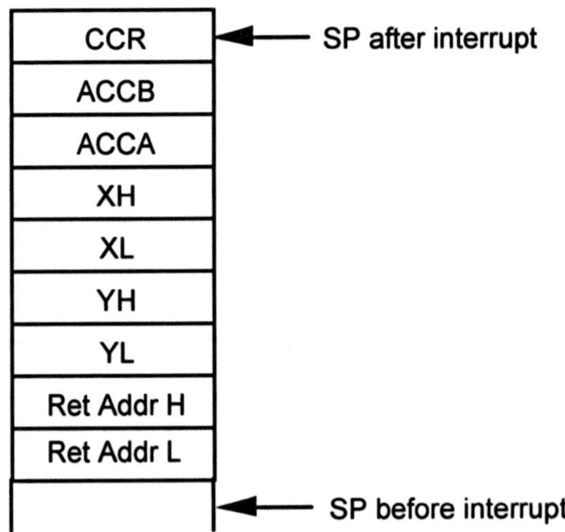

Figure B.9 Register stacking for interrupts

B.5.2 68HC12 Maskable Interrupts

All of the interrupts shown in Appendix D with vector numbers between 6 and 57 are maskable interrupts that are inhibited when the *I* bit in the *CCR* is set (using the *SEI* instruction). To enable all of these maskable interrupts you must clear the *I* bit in the *CCR* by executing the *CLI* instruction. In addition, each interrupt source will have a local enable bit that must be set in one of the I/O registers in order to enable that particular interrupt. For example, to enable pin *PE1* as an IRQ interrupt, you must set bit *IRQEN* (bit 6) in the *Interrupt Control Register, INTCR.*

The interrupts shown in Appendix D are listed in order of priority. If more than one interrupt occurs at the same time, the interrupt with the highest priority will be serviced first.

When maskable interrupts occur the same process of pushing the registers on the stack occurs as described above for software interrupts.

Appendix C

Summary of C Function Calls to *main.asm*

Example 1: C function calls for turning on the 7-segment display

C Function Call	Meaning
`seg7_enable();`	Sets DDRH to outputs and clears all segments
`seg7_on(int);`	Stores the lower 8 bits of the integer *int* in Port H
`seg7_off();`	Turn off all 7 segments by clearing Port H

Example 2: C function call delaying *n* milliseconds

C Function Call	Meaning
`ms_delay(int n);`	Delay *n* milliseconds

Example 3: C function call for displaying digit on 7-segment display

C Function Call	Meaning
`seg7dec(int i);`	Display the hex digit *i* on the 7-segment display

Example 4: C function calls for turning on or off a single bit of PTH

C Function Call	Meaning
`PTH_HI(int b);`	Sets bit *b* of PTH high
`PTH_LO(int b);`	Sets bit *b* of PTH low

Example 5: C function calls for reading switches S1 and S2

C Function Call	Meaning
`SW12_enable();`	Enable switches S1 and S2
`SW1_down();`	Returns **true** if S1 is down
`SW2_down();`	Returns **true** if S2 is down
`SW1_up();`	Returns **true** if S1 is up
`SW2_up();`	Returns **true** if S2 is up

Example 6: C function calls for reading a 4 x 4 keypad

C Function Call	Meaning
`keypad_enable();`	Enable the keypad
`int getkey();`	Waits to press key and returns value
`void wait_keyup();`	Waits until key is not being pressed
`int keyscan();`	Returns 16 if no key is being pressed Returns key value if key is being pressed

Example 7: C Function calls for LCD display

Function	Description
`void lcd_init(void);`	Initialize LCD display (clears display)
`void set_lcd_addr(char);`	Set cursor address (see Fig. 6.3)
`void data8(char);`	Write ASCII character to display at cursor location
`void instr8(char);`	Write instruction to display (see Table 6.1)
`void clear_lcd(void);`	Clear LCD display
`void hex2lcd(char);`	Write hex digit (0 – F) to LCD display
`char hex2asc(char);`	Convert hex digit (0 – F) to ASCII code
`void type_lcd(char*);`	Display ASCIIZ string on LCD display at cursor location

Example 8: C Function calls for the SCI port

Function	Description
`void SCI0_init(int b);`	Initialize SCI0 with baud rate *b*
`char inchar0(void);`	Wait for character in SCI0 and return char
`void outchar0(char c);`	Output character *c* out SCI0 TxD pin
`void SCI1_init(int b);`	Initialize SCI1 with baud rate *b*
`char inchar1(void);`	Wait for character in SCI1 and return char
`void outchar1(char c);`	Output character *c* out SCI1 TxD pin

Example 9: C function calls for writing integers to the LCD

C Function Call	**Meaning**
`void write_int_lcd(int);`	Display 16-bit integer right-justified in a field of 5 digits
`void write_long_lcd(long);`	Display 32-bit integer right-justified in a field of 10 digits

Example 10: C Function call for converting ASCII number string to binary

Function	Description
`long number(char* ptr);`	Return 32-bit number equal to ASCII number string

Example 11: C Function calls for the A/D converters

Function	Description
`void ad0_enable(void);`	Enable ATD0 for 10 bits
`int ad0conv(char ch#);`	Return the avg of 4 successive readings of channel *ch#*
`void ad1_enable(void);`	Enable ATD1 for 10 bits
`int ad1conv(char ch#);`	Return the avg of 4 successive readings of channel *ch#*

Example 12: C function calls for controlling the position of a servo

C Function Call	**Meaning**
`servo54_init();`	Initialize PWM5 with 20 ms period
`servo76_init();`	Initialize PWM7 with 20 ms period
`set_servo54(int width);`	Set position of servo5 (3300 – 5700)
`set_servo76(int width);`	Set position of servo7 (3300 – 5700)

Example 12: C function calls for controlling the speed of a DC motor

C Function Call	Meaning
void **motor0_init**(void);	Initialize PWM0 with 10 ms period
void **motor1_init**(void);	Initialize PWM1 with 10 ms period
void **motor2_init**(void);	Initialize PWM2 with 10 ms period
void **motor3_init**(void);	Initialize PWM3 with 10 ms period
void **motor4_init**(void);	Initialize PWM4 with 10 ms period
void **motor5_init**(void);	Initialize PWM5 with 10 ms period
void **motor6_init**(void);	Initialize PWM6 with 10 ms period
void **motor7_init**(void);	Initialize PWM7 with 10 ms period
void **motor0**(int speed);	Set speed of motor0 (0 – 255)
void **motor1**(int speed);	Set speed of motor1 (0 – 255)
void **motor2**(int speed);	Set speed of motor2 (0 – 255)
void **motor3**(int speed);	Set speed of motor3 (0 – 255)
void **motor4**(int speed);	Set speed of motor4 (0 – 255)
void **motor5**(int speed);	Set speed of motor5 (0 – 255)
void **motor6**(int speed);	Set speed of motor6 (0 – 255)
void **motor7**(int speed);	Set speed of motor7 (0 – 255)

Example 13: C Function calls for the SPI ports

Function	Description
void **SPI0_init**(void);	Initialize SPI0 with baud rate of 250 KHz
char **send_SPI0**(char c);	Send character *c* out SCI0; returns character shifted in
void **SS0_HI**(void);	Set SS0 (PS7, pin 95) HI
void **SS0_LO**(void);	Set SS0 (PS7, pin 95) LO
void **SPI1_init**();	Initialize SPI1 with baud rate of 250 KHz
char **send_SPI1**(char c);	Send character *c* out SCI1; returns character shifted in
void **SS1_HI**(void);	Set SS1 (PP3, pin 1) HI
void **SS1_LO**(void);	Set SS1 (PP3, pin 1) LO
void **SPI2_init**();	Initialize SPI2 with baud rate of 250 KHz
char **send_SPI2**(char c);	Send character *c* out SCI2; returns character shifted in
void **SS2_HI**(void);	Set SS2 (PP6, pin 110) HI
void **SS2_LO**(void);	Set SS2 (PP6, pin 110) LO

Example 14: C Function calls for the real-time interrupt

Function	Description
void **RTI_init**(void);	Initialize real-time interrupts every 10.24 ms
void **clear_RTI_flag**(void)	Clear the RTI flag
void **RTI_disable**(void)	Disable real-time interrupts

Example 17: C Function calls for the SCI port with interrupts

Function	Description
void **SCI0_int_init**(int b);	Initialize SCI0 with interrupts and baud rate *b*
char **read_SCI0_Rx**(void);	Read character received in SCI0 Rx port
void **outchar0**(char c);	Output character *c* out SCI0 TxD pin
void **SCI1_int_init**(int b);	Initialize SCI1 with interrupts and baud rate *b*
char **read_SCI1_Rx**(void);	Read character received in SCI1 Rx port
void **outchar1**(char c);	Output character *c* out SCI1 TxD pin

Example 18: C Function calls for generating a pulse train

Function	Description
`void ptrain6_init(void);`	initialize pulse train interrupts on PT6 timer clock = 1.5 MHz
`void ptrain6(int period, int pwidth);`	update TC6 and TC7 in timer 6 interrupt routine
`void sound_init(void);`	initialize pulse train interrupts on PT5 (speaker) timer clock = 1.5 MHz
`void sound_on(void);`	Turn sound on by enabling timer and interrupts
`void sound_off(void);`	Turn sound off by disabling timer and interrupts
`void tone(int pitch);`	Set pitch value of sound by updating TC5 and TC7 in timer 5 interrupt routine

Example 19: C Function calls for measuring pulse widths on Channel 1

Function	Description
`void HILO1_init(void);`	initialize input capture interrupts on both edges of channel 1; timer clock = 1.5 MHz
`void HILOtimes1(void);`	update HI – LO times in input capture interrupt routine
`int get_HItime1(void);`	return latest HI time of input pulse train
`int get_LOtime1(void);`	return latest LO time of input pulse train

Example 21: C function calls for a fuzzy controller

C Function Call	**Meaning**
`void fill_weights(unsigned char* weight, unsigned char* membx, int num_mem_fncs, char x);`	Given a crisp input *x* and membership functions, *membx*, fill the corresponding *weight* array.
`void fire_rules(unsigned char* inout_array, unsigned char* rules, unsigned char* out, int numout);`	Given *inout_array* containing *weight* arrays and a set of *rules*, fire all rules and fill the *out* array.
`unsigned char calc_output(unsigned char* out, unsigned char* cent, int numout);`	Calculate crisp output given the *out* array and the output membership singletons, *cent*.

Function Calls to *queue.c*

Example 17: C Function calls for using the character queue in queue.c

Function	Description
`void initq(void);`	initialize the queue
`void qstore(char);`	store character in queue
`int qempty(void);`	return 0 if queue is not empty
`char getq(void);`	read character from queue

Appendix D

MC9S12DP256B Interrupt Vectors

Vector Number	Interrupt Source	Vector Address
0	Reset	$FFFE-$FFFF
1	Clock Monitor Fail Reset	$FFFC-$FFFD
2	COP Failure Reset	$FFFA-$FFFB
3	Unimplemented Instruction Trap	$FFF8-$FFF9
4	SWI	$FFF6-$FFF7
5	XIRQ	$FFF4-$FFF5
6	IRQ	$FFF2-$FFF3
7	Real-Time Interrupt	$FFF0-$FFF1
8	Timer Channel 0	$FFEE-$FFEF
9	Timer Channel 1	$FFEC-$FFED
10	Timer Channel 2	$FFEA-$FFEB
11	Timer Channel 3	$FFE8-$FFE9
12	Timer Channel 4	$FFE6-$FFE7
13	Timer Channel 5	$FFE4-$FFE5
14	Timer Channel 6	$FFE2-$FFE3
15	Timer Channel 7	$FFE0-$FFE1
16	Timer Overflow	$FFDE-$FFDF
17	Pulse Accumulator A Overflow	$FFDC-$FFDD
18	Pulse Accumulator Input Edge	$FFDA-$FFDB
19	SPI0	$FFD8-$FFD9
20	SCI 0	$FFD6-$FFD7
21	SCI 1	$FFD4-$FFD5
22	ATD0	$FFD2-$FFD3
23	ATD1	$FFD0-$FFD1
24	Port J	$FFCE-$FFCF
25	Port H	$FFCC-$FFCD
26	Modulus Down Counter Underflow	$FFCA-$FFCB
27	Pulse Accumulator B Overflow	$FFC8-$FFC9
28	CRG PLL lock	$FFC6-$FFC7
29	CRG Self Clock Mode	$FFC4-$FFC5
30	BDLC	$FFC2-$FFC3
31	IIC Bus	$FFC0-$FFC1
32	SPI1	$FFBE-$FFBF
33	SPI2	$FFBC-$FFBD
34	EEPROM	$FFBA-$FFBB
35	FLASH	$FFB8-$FFB9

36	CAN0 wake-up	$FFB6-$FFB7
37	CAN0 errors	$FFB4-$FFB5
38	CAN0 receive	$FFB2-$FFB3
39	CAN0 transmit	$FFB0-$FFB1
40	CAN1 wake-up	$FFAE-$FFAF
41	CAN1 errors	$FFAC-$FFAD
42	CAN1 receive	$FFAA-$FFAB
43	CAN1 transmit	$FFA8-$FFA9
44	CAN2 wake-up	$FFA6-$FFA7
45	CAN2 errors	$FFA4-$FFA5
46	CAN2 receive	$FFA2-$FFA3
47	CAN2 transmit	$FFA0-$FFA1
48	CAN3 wake-up	$FF9E-$FF9F
49	CAN3 errors	$FF9C-$FF9D
50	CAN3 receive	$FF9A-$FF9B
51	CAN3 transmit	$FF98-$FF99
52	CAN4 wake-up	$FF96-$FF97
53	CAN4 errors	$FFA4-$FF95
54	CAN4 receive	$FF92-$FF93
55	CAN4 transmit	$FF90-$FF91
56	Port P Interrupt	$FF8E-$FF8F
57	PWM Emergency Shutdown	$FF8C-$FF8D
	Reserved	$FF80-$FF8B

Appendix E

Introduction to Fuzzy Control

Fuzzy logic has been applied successfully to a wide variety of difficult control problems. The input and output control variables are members of fuzzy sets that admit varying degrees of membership. In this appendix we will introduce the basic ideas of fuzzy sets. We will then describe how a fuzzy controller works and present an overall approach to implementing a fuzzy controller on a microcontroller. The HCS12 has some special instructions which simplify the implementation of a fuzzy controller. We define some C functions in Example 20 that use these HCS12 instructions to implement a fuzzy controller.

E.1 Fuzzy Sets

Lotfi Zadeh introduced the term *fuzzy sets* in 1965.* In normal "crisp" logic the basic assumption is that assertions, or statements, are either *true* or *false*. But this assumption leads to paradoxes. For example, is the sentence in Figure E.1 true or false? If the sentence is true, then it must be false; but if it is false, then it must be true. There are many such paradoxes in which it appears that true must be equal to false.

The sentence on the other side of the line is false
The sentence on the other side of the line is false

Figure E.1 Is this sentence *true* of *false*?

Fuzzy logic does not require that everything be either true or false. In normal "crisp" set theory an element either belongs to the set, or it doesn't. However, a little

* L. Zadeh, "Fuzzy Sets," Inform. and Contr., Vol. 8, pp. 338-353, 1965.

reflection should convince you that most things in the world aren't that black and white. For example, is a given person *young*? We can consider *young* to be a fuzzy set in which we use membership functions to define the degree of membership (between 0 and 1) in the set.

A membership function for the fuzzy set *Young* is shown in Figure E.2. People who are younger than age *a1* are definitely young (with a degree of membership equal to 1) while people who are older than age *a2* are definitely not young (with a degree of membership equal to 0). However, people with ages between *a1* and *a2* are young to some degree determined by the membership function shown in Figure E.2.

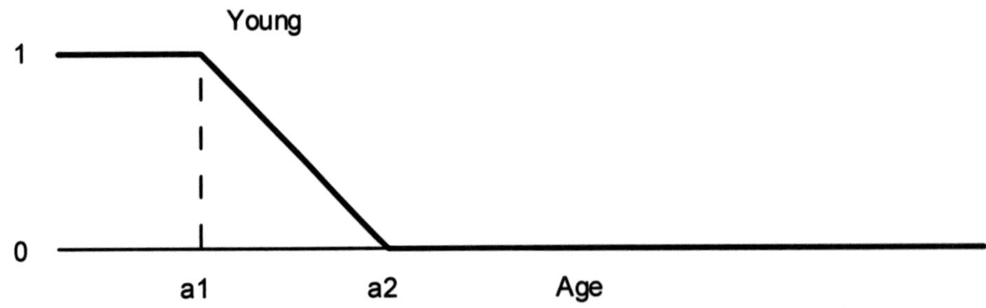

Figure E.2 Membership function for the fuzzy set *Young*

When applied to fuzzy sets the logic operations *NOT*, *AND*, and *OR* are defined as shown in Table E.1. These are not the only possible definitions but they are the ones most commonly used. Note that they reduce to the crisp case when *A* and *B* have the binary values 0 and 1.

Table E.1 Fuzzy Logic Operations

Logic Operation	Fuzzy Logic Operation
NOT a	1 - a
a AND b	MIN(a,b)
a OR b	MAX(a,b)

If we apply the *NOT* operation to the fuzzy set *Young* we obtain the fuzzy set *NOT Young* shown in Figure E.3. In a similar way we could define the fuzzy sets *Old* and *NOT Old* as shown in Figure E.4.

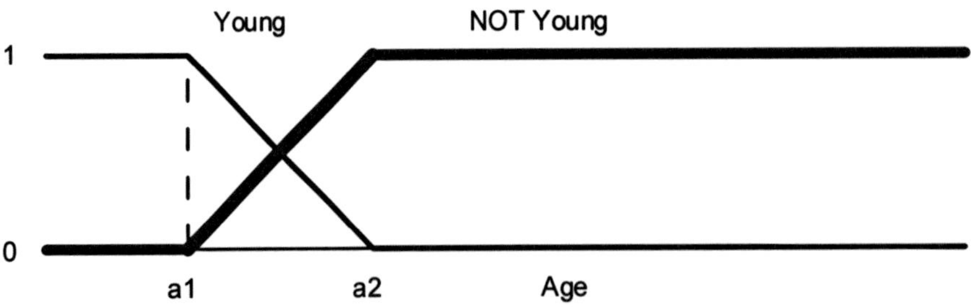

Figure E.3 *NOT Young* = 1 - *Young*

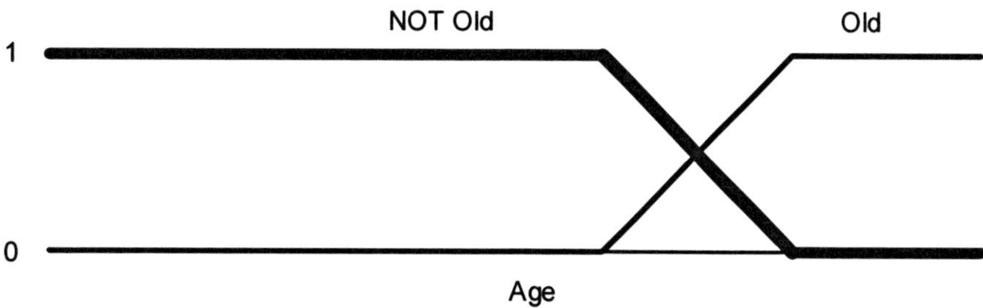

Figure E.4 Membership functions for the fuzzy sets *Old* and *NOT Old*

We can use the *AND* operation given in Table E.1 to define new fuzzy sets. For example, we might define *Middle Age* as *NOT Young AND Not Old.* Taking the minimum of the membership functions for *NOT Young* and *NOT Old* will produce the membership function for *Middle Age* as shown in Figure E.5.

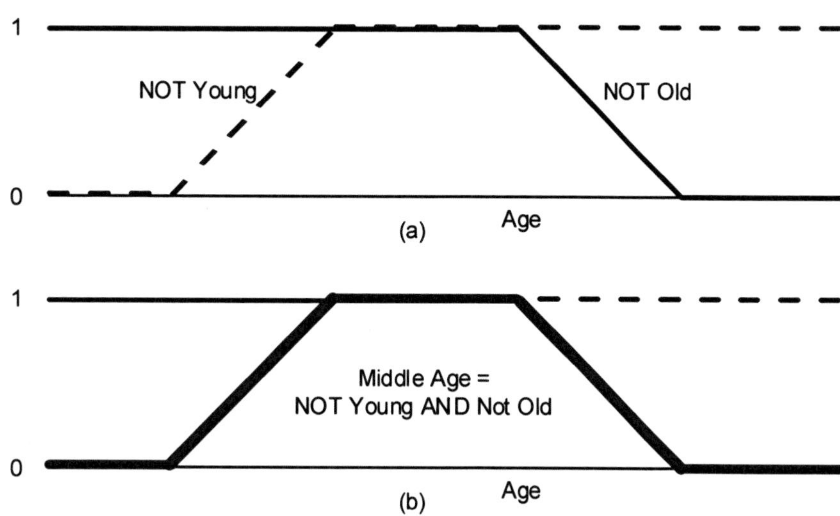

Figure E.5 Deriving the membership function for *Middle Age*

E.2 Design of a Fuzzy Controller

In this section we will show how fuzzy logic can be applied to the control of physical systems. The design process begins by associating fuzzy sets with the input and output variables. These fuzzy sets are described by membership functions of the type shown in Figure E.6. These fuzzy set values are labeled *NM* (negative medium), *NS* (negative small), *Z* (zero), *PS* (positive small), and *PM* (positive medium). For example, if an input variable is temperature, the five membership functions might be labeled *COLD*, *COOL*, *MEDIUM*, *WARM*, and *HOT*. The shape of the membership functions are, in general, trapezoids that may have no top (triangles) or may have vertical sides as shown in Figure E.6.

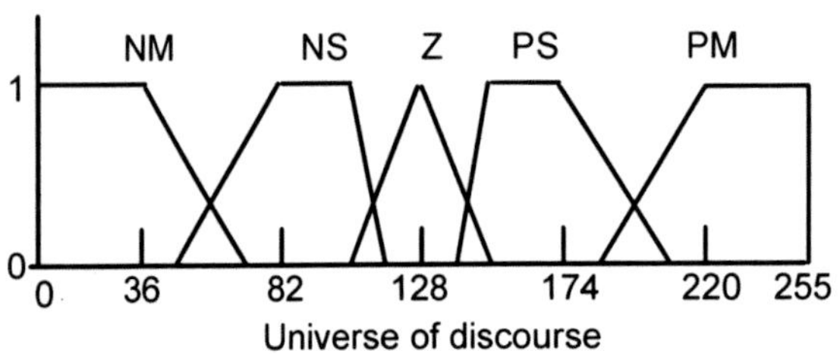

Figure E.6 Example of fuzzy membership functions

A functional diagram of a fuzzy controller is shown in Figure E.7. The inputs to a fuzzy controller are assigned to the fuzzy variables with a degree of membership given by the membership functions. For example, in Figure E.6 an input value of 140 would have a degree of membership of 0.25 in *Z* and a degree of membership of 0.5 in *PS*. On the other hand, an input value of 85 would belong to *NS* with a degree of membership of 1.0. In general, an input value will belong to all fuzzy sets with different degrees of membership (including zero).

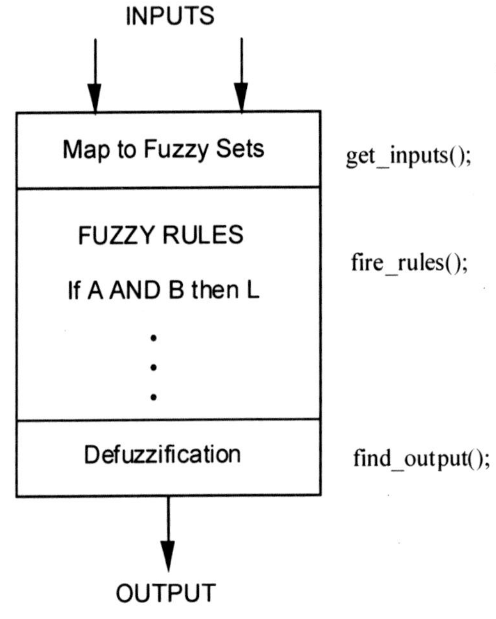

Figure E.7 Functional diagram of a fuzzy controller

The fuzzy controller itself consists of a set of fuzzy rules of the form *if* x_1 *is PM AND* x_2 *is Z, then y is NM*, where x_1 and x_2 are inputs, *y* is the output, and *PM*, *Z* and *NM* are fuzzy sets of the type shown in Figure E.6. For example, a fuzzy rule for an air conditioner might be *if temperature is WARM AND change in temperature is ZERO, then motor speed is FAST*. Note that *WARM*, *ZERO*, and *FAST* are fuzzy sets. After applying all of the fuzzy rules to a given set of input variables, the output (motor speed in this case) will, in general, belong to more than one fuzzy set with different weights. The weighted output fuzzy sets are combined in a manner to be described below and then a centroid defuzzification process is used to obtain a single crisp output value.

The fuzzy controller shown in Figure E.7 consists of three parts: the fuzzification of inputs, the processing of rules, and the defuzzification of the output. The overall algorithm of a fuzzy controller is shown in Figure E.8 where each function represents the three parts of the controller shown in Figure E.7. We will consider each of these parts separately.

```
do_forever
        {
        get_inputs();
        fire_rules();
        find_output();
        }
```

Figure E.8 Overall algorithm of a fuzzy controller

E.3 Fuzzification of Inputs

For each crisp input x_i a set of weights w_j^i are computed for each membership function such as those shown in Figure E.6. In general, each input will have a different set and number of membership functions. For input number i the weight w_j^i can be stored in a vector $weight_i[j]$, $j = 1, M_i$ where M_i is the number of membership functions for input i. Each value in the weight vector is a weight value between 0 and 1 given by the shape of a particular membership function. Typically for a given input the weight vector will contain up to two non-zero entries in adjacent cells.

The purpose of the function *get_inputs()* is to read each input value x_i and fill the weight vector $weight[M_i]$ with the degree of membership of x_i in each input fuzzy set. The pseudo-code for *get_inputs()* is shown in Figure E.9. In this figure M_i is the number of membership functions for input i.

```
get_inputs()
for i = 1, num_inputs
        {
        get_x(i);
        fill_weight(xi, Mi);
        }
```

Figure E.9 Pseudocode for *get_inputs()*

The function *get_x(i)* is problem dependent and will consist of reading the input values x_i, $i = 1$, *num_inputs*. The function $fill\_weight(x_i, M_i)$ will fill the weight vector $weight[M_i]$ with the degree of membership of x_i in each of the M_i membership functions for input i.

E.4 Fuzzy Inference

The heart of a fuzzy controller is the list of fuzzy rules. Fuzzy logic inference is used to find a fuzzy output, given a fuzzy input and a list of fuzzy rules. In a fuzzy controller the inputs are normally crisp, non-fuzzy values that must first be fuzzified in the first step of Figure E.7 as described in Section E.3. The output also needs to be a crisp value used to control some device. Therefore, the fuzzy output resulting from processing the fuzzy rules must be defuzzified as described in the next section. The way fuzzy rules are processed is illustrated in Figure E.10 where fuzzy sets are represented by their membership functions *m*.

Fuzzy inference involves a set of fuzzy rules of the form

if x_1 is A_1 and x_2 is B_1 then y is L_1 rule 1

if x_1 is A_2 and x_2 is B_2 then y is L_2 rule 2

Given the fact that

x_1 is A' and x_2 is B' fact

the problem is to find the conclusion

y is L' conclusion

In this representation of the problem, A_1, A_2, B_1, B_2, A', and B' are input fuzzy sets and L_1, L_2, and L' are output fuzzy sets. Fuzzy reasoning would form the union of the intersection of A' and A_1. This is interpreted as being the maximum (union) of the minimum (intersection) of the membership functions A' and A_1. In Figure E.10 A' is taken to be the singleton fuzzy set $x_1 = a$. In rule 1, the maximum of the intersection (minimum) of this singleton with A_1 is the value w_1 shown in Figure E.10. Similarly, the maximum of the intersection (minimum) of the singleton $x_2 = b$ with B_1 is the value w_2 shown in Figure E.10. The fact $x_1 = a$ *and* $x_2 = b$ applied to the antecedent x_1 *is* A_1 *and* x_2 *is* B_1 is interpreted as the intersection (minimum) of w_1 and w_2, i.e. w_2 for rule 1 in Figure E.10. The conclusion of rule 1, y *is* L_1, is found by taking the intersection (T-norm) of w_2 with L_1. This is normally the minimum operation which would truncate L_1 to the height w_2. However, for fuzzy control it is sometimes advantageous to use a product T-norm for this intersection which would have the effect of multiplying L_1 by w_2 as shown in rule 1 in Figure E.10. Thus, rule 1 in Figure E.10 will contribute the fuzzy set $w_2 * L_1$ to the conclusion fuzzy set L'. Similarly, rule 2 in Figure E.10 will contribute the fuzzy set $w_1 * L_2$ to the conclusion fuzzy set L' because w_1 is the minimum of w_1 and w_2 for rule 2. Note that if L_1 and L_2 are singletons (as is normally the case) then there will be no difference in using the minimum T-norm or the product T-norm.

The conclusion fuzzy set L' is found by forming the T-conorm of $w_2 * L_1$ and $w_1 * L_2$. This is normally the maximum operation. However, sometimes better results are obtained by taking the sum of $w_2 * L_1$ and $w_1 * L_2$ as shown in Figure E.10. The difference between these two approaches is shown in Figure E.11.

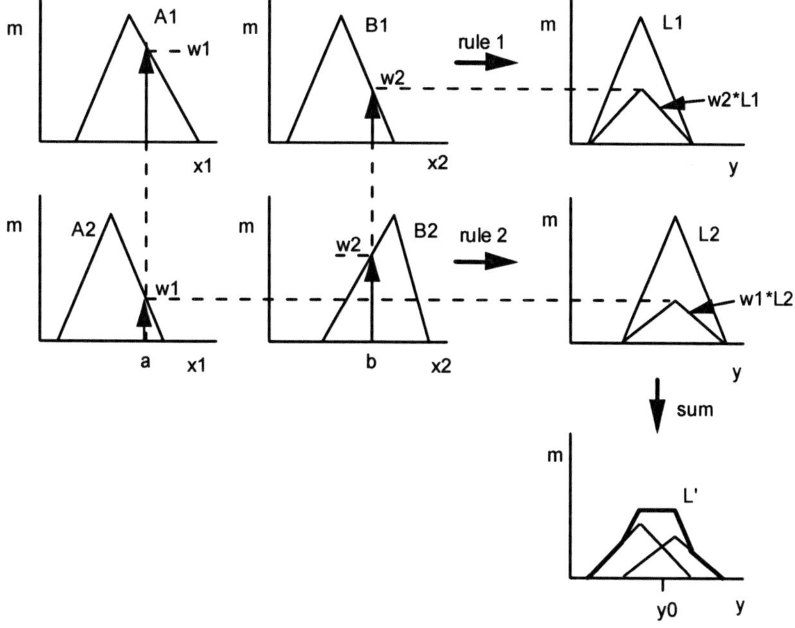

Figure E.10 Fuzzy inference

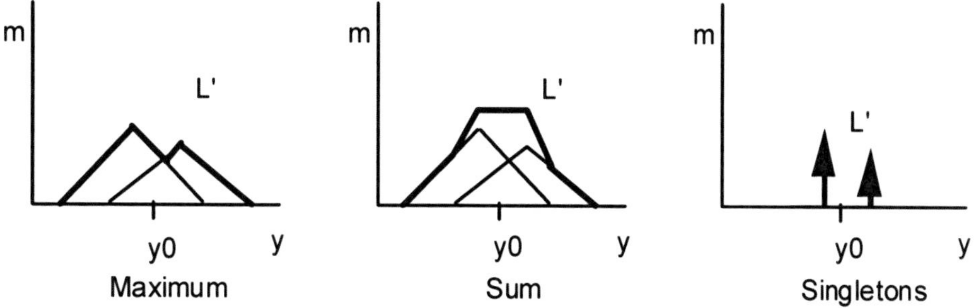

Figure E.11 Comparing the MAX rule and the SUM rule

If L_1 and L_2 are singletons (the normal case) then taking the maximum or sum of the two rules shown in Figure E.10 will be the same as shown in Figure E.11. In general, they won't be the same if more than one rule contribute to the same output fuzzy set L_i. In this case the maximum rule will keep only the maximum value while the sum rule will add the contributions of each.

The conclusion output L' is a fuzzy set shown by the bold line membership function in Figures E.10 and E.11. To obtain a crisp output some type of defuzzification process is required. The most common method is to compute the centroid of the area of L'. We will see that using the sum rule will be helpful in analyzing centroid defuzzification in Section E.5.

E.5 Centroid Defuzzification

The last step in the fuzzy controller shown in Figure E.7 is defuzzification. This involves finding the centroid of the net output fuzzy set L' shown in Figures E.10 and E.11. Although we have used the MIN-MAX rule in the previous section we will begin by deriving the centroid equation for the sum rule shown in Figure E.11. This will illuminate the assumptions made in deriving the defuzzification equation that we will actually use in the fuzzy controller.

Let $L_i(y)$ be the original output membership function associated with rule i where y is the output universe of discourse (see Figure E.10.). After applying rule i this membership function will be reduced to the value

$$m_i(y) = w_i L_i(y) \tag{E.1}$$

where w_i is the minimum weight found by applying rule i. The sum of these reduced output membership functions over all rules is then given by

$$M(y) = \sum_{i=1}^{N} m_i(y) \tag{E.2}$$

where N is the number of rules.

The crisp output value y_0 is then given by the centroid of $M(y)$ from the equation

$$y_0 = \frac{\int y M(y) dy}{\int M(y) dy} \tag{E.3}$$

Note that the centroid of membership function $L_i(y)$ is given by

$$c_i = \frac{\int y L_i(y) dy}{\int L_i(y) dy} \tag{E.4}$$

But

$$I_i = \int L_i(y) dy \tag{E.5}$$

is just the area of membership function $L_i(y)$. Substituting (E.5) into (E.4) we can write

$$\int y L_i(y) dy = c_i I_i \tag{E.6}$$

Using Eqs. (E.1) and (E.2) we can write the numerator of (E.3) as

$$\int yM(y)dy = \int y \sum_{i=1}^{N} w_i L_i(y)\, dy$$

$$= \sum_{i=1}^{N} \int y w_i L_i(y)\, dy$$

$$= \sum_{i=1}^{N} w_i c_i I_i \qquad \text{(E.7)}$$

where (E.6) was used in the last step.
Similarly, using (E.1) and (E.2) the denominator of (E.3) can be written as

$$\int M(y)dy = \int \sum_{i=1}^{N} w_i L_i(y)\, dy$$

$$= \sum_{i=1}^{N} \int w_i L_i(y)\, dy$$

$$= \sum_{i=1}^{N} w_i I_i \qquad \text{(E.8)}$$

where (E.5) was used in the last step. Substituting (E.7) and (E.8) into (E.3) we can write the crisp output of the fuzzy controller as

$$y_0 = \frac{\sum_{i=1}^{N} w_i c_i I_i}{\sum_{i=1}^{N} w_i I_i} \qquad \text{(E.9)}$$

Eq. (E.9) says that we can compute the output centroid from the centroids, c_i, of the individual output membership functions.

Note in Eq. (E.9) the summation is over all N rules. But the number of output membership functions, Q, will, in general, be less than the number of rules, N. This means that in the sums in Eq. (E.9) there will be many terms that will have the same values of c_i and I_i. For example, suppose that rules 2, 3, and 4 in the sum all have the output membership function L^k as the consequent. This means that in the sum

$$w_2 c_2 I_2 + w_3 c_3 I_3 + w_4 c_4 I_4$$

the values c_i and I_i are the same values c^k and I^k because they are just the centroid and area of the kth output membership function. These three terms would then contribute the value

$$(w_2 + w_3 + w_4)c^k I^k = W^k c^k I^k$$

to the sum, where

$$W^k = (w_2 + w_3 + w_4)$$

is the sum of all weights from rules whose consequent is output membership function L^k. This means that the equation for the output value, y_0, given by (E.9) can be rewritten as

$$y_0 = \frac{\sum_{k=1}^{Q} W^k c^k I^k}{\sum_{k=1}^{Q} W^k I^k} \tag{E.10}$$

If the area of all output membership functions, I^k are equal, then Eq. (E.10) reduces to

$$y_0 = \frac{\sum_{k=1}^{Q} W^k c^k}{\sum_{k=1}^{Q} W^k} \tag{E.11}$$

Eqs. (E.10) and (E.11) show that the output crisp value of a fuzzy controller can be computed by summing over only the number of output membership functions rather than over all fuzzy rules. Also, if we use Eq. (E.11) to compute the output crisp value, then we need to specify only the centroids, c^k, of the output fuzzy membership functions. This is equivalent to assuming singleton fuzzy sets for the output.

For more information on fuzzy control you can consult the many books on this topic including

Fuzzy Logic and Control: Software and Hardware Applications, Vol. 2, by M. Jamshidi, N. Vadiee, and T. Ross, Prentice-Hall, Upper Saddle River, NJ, 1993.

Applications of Fuzzy Logic: Towards High Machine Intelligence Quotient Systems, by M. Jamshidi, A. Titli, L. Zadeh, and S. Boverie, Prentice-Hall, Upper Saddle River, NJ, 1997.

Appendix F

C Quick Reference Guide

Category	Definition	Example

Identifer Names	Can contain any letter, digit, or underscore _
	Can not begin with a digit or be a keyword
	Case sensitive
		`q3`
		`SCI0_init`
		`val32`

Integer Numbers	signed char (8 bit) -128 to + 127
	unsigned char (8 bit) 0 to 255
	short (16 bit) -32,768 to +32,767
	unsigned short (16 bit) 0 to 65,535
	int (16 bit) -32,768 to +32,767
	unsigned int (16 bit) 0 to 65,535
	long (32 bit) -2,147,483,648 to +2,147,483,647
	unsigned long (32 bit) 0 to 4,294,967,295
		`char c`
		`unsigned char x3`
		`short Jay`
		`unsigned short ticks`
		`int i`
		`unsigned int Green`
		`long var32`
		`unsigned long Black`

Real Numbers (floating point)	float (32 bits) 6 significant digits double (64 bits) 10 significant digits long double (64 bits) 10 significant digits	`float radius` `double rose`

Constants	Decimal
	
	Hexadecimal (Hex)
		`1234`
		`55`
		`0xFC`
		`0xA4C9`

Characters	char	`char c`

Constant character arrays	Used to build a table of constant values	`const char seg7tbl[] = {`
		`0x3F,0x06,0x5B,0x4f,`
		`0x66,0x6D,0x7D,0x07,`
		`0x7F,0x6F,0x77,0x7C,`
		`0x39,0x5E,0x79,0x71`
		`};`

Character strings	"This is a string"	`char* q1;`
		`char* q2;`
		`q1 = "Programming";`
		`q2 = "Microcontrollers";`

Arrays	A named collection of values of a particular type.	`unsigned char memb_speed[20]`
		`unsigned char cent[ ] = {`
		`5,65,128,175,220`
		`};`
		`memb_speed[j+2] = 0;`
		`x = cent[2];`

Pointers	An address that points to some memory location.	`char* ptr;`
		`char* plus;`
		`char kbuf[12];`
		`ptr = kbuf;`
		`plus = "+ ";`

Arithmetic operators	+ (addition) - (subtraction) * (multiplication) / (division) % (mod)	`count = count + 1;` `count++`

C Quick Reference Guide (cont.)

<table>
<tr><td>Relational operators</td><td>==, !=, >, <, >=, <=, ===, !==</td><td>while(a <= b);
if(clr == 1)</td></tr>
<tr><td>Logic operators</td><td>! (Logical negation)
&& (Logical AND)
|| (Logical OR)
& (Bitwise AND)
| (Bitwise OR)
^ (Bitwise Exclusive OR)</td><td>while((i < 16) && (found == 0)){
if((data & mask) == 0){
found = 1;
key = keytbl[i];
}
else {
mask >>= 1;
i++;
}
}</td></tr>
<tr><td>Shift operators</td><td><< (shift left)
>> (shift right)</td><td>speed = val >> 2;
data = data << 8;</td></tr>
<tr><td>Shorthand operators</td><td>++ (increment)
-- (decrement)
+= a += b same as a = a + b
-=, *=. /= %=
<<=. >>=, ^= &=, |=</td><td>ticks++;
i--;
a += 5;
data |= c;
PTH &= 0xFE;
mask >>= 1;</td></tr>
<tr><td>Functions</td><td>return_type function_name(param1, …parmN){
local_declarations;
statements;
}</td><td>void qstore(char c){
rear++;
if(rear > max)
rear = min;
if(rear == front){
rear--;
if(rear < min)
rear = max;
}else
qbuff[rear] = c;
}
char getq(void){
front++;
if(front > max)
front = 0;
return qbuff[front];
}</td></tr>
<tr><td>Main program</td><td>preprocessor statements

void main(void) {
declarations;
statements;
}</td><td>void main(void) {
PLL_init();
DDRH = 0xff;
PTH = 0x55;
while(1) {
}
}</td></tr>
<tr><td>if statement</td><td>if(expression){
statement;
else
statement;
}</td><td>if(readback == keycodes[i]){
key = i;
found = 1;
}
else
i++;</td></tr>
<tr><td>for loop</td><td>for(initial_index; terminal_index; increment)
statement;</td><td>for(i = 0; i < 16; i++){
PORTB = seg7tbl[i];
delay();
}</td></tr>
<tr><td>while loop</td><td>while(expression)
statement;</td><td>while(SW1_down()){
seg7dec(1);
}</td></tr>
</table>

C Quick Reference Guide (cont.)

switch statement	**switch**(expression) {
	case alternative1:
	statements;
	break;
	case alternative2:
	statements;
	break;
	default:
	statements;
	break;
	}
		switch(c){
		case 0xE:
		set_lcd_addr(0x40);
		while(qempty() != 0){
		data8(getq());
		}
		set_lcd_addr(0x00);
		type_lcd(blanks);
		wait_keyup();
		set_lcd_addr(0x00);
		break;
		case 0xF:
		clear_lcd();
		wait_keyup();
		break;
		default:
		break;
		}

static storage class	A static local variable will retain its value from call to call. A static global variable is not visible to other program files.	**static char** qbuff[QMAX]; **static int** front; **static int** rear;

Interrupts	void interrupt <vector_number> int_name() {
	statements;
	}
		void interrupt 7 handler(){
		ticks++;
		clear_RTI_flag();
		}

Index

CPSIA information can be obtained at www.ICGtesting.com
Printed in the USA
BVOW04s2002170915

418524BV00001B/1/P

9 780980 133721